William James Adams

Hints on Amalgamation and the general care of Gold Mills

William James Adams

Hints on Amalgamation and the general care of Gold Mills

ISBN/EAN: 9783337058951

Printed in Europe, USA, Canada, Australia, Japan

Cover: Foto ©ninafisch / pixelio.de

More available books at **www.hansebooks.com**

HINTS

— ON —

AMALGAMATION

AND THE

GENERAL CARE OF GOLD MILLS

BY

W. J. ADAMS, A. M., E. M.

Graduate of the School of Mines of Columbia University,
New York.

A Reference Book of Actual Gold-Mill Practice, as
Determined by an Experience of Twenty Years
Written in Language that can be
Understood by All.

ILLUSTRATED.

CHICAGO:
MODERN MACHINERY PUBLISHING COMPANY.
1899.

Entered According to Act of Congress in the Year 1898,
BY W. J. ADAMS.
In the Office of the Librarian of Congress at Washington, D. C.

TABLE OF CONTENTS.

	Page.
Introduction	7
Chapter 1—General Process	11
Arrangement of Mortars	17
" " Plates	21
" " Concentrators	30
" " for Canvas Plant	34
" 2—Care of Quicksilver	35
Amalgamation	43
" 3—Cleaning-up	60
" 4—Retorting and Melting	73
" 5—Concentration	85
" 6—Sampling	98
" 7—Conclusion	108

INTRODUCTION.

Gold has been known from the earliest ages, from its occurrence in a metallic state in sedimentary deposits as well as in veins. On account of its great specific gravity, it can be collected from placers and river beds, by separation with water alone, and in veins after the matrix is crushed, a great amount is saved by the same simple method. When only rich deposits were exploited, anybody could manage as it apparently required only labor and opportunity, while as long as money was made, the losses that occurred did not trouble the owners. From this very simplicity of working, the majority of owners and investors imagined that no special training was requisite to insure success, but that any trustworthy man, skilled in mercantile pursuits, was the proper person for the place of general manager. To-day the same opinion is held by very many, in spite of the warnings from hosts of disastrous failures. One cause for this belief has been the lack of literature for this special branch of metallurgy; in fact, very near 1890, there was practically no works written at all which spoke of gold except as a subsidiary product of the metallurgy of other metals. Volumes, both practical and scientific, have been published which deal with the special branches of the metallurgy of lead, copper, and silver, but the metallurgy of gold seemed so simple, it only required an occasional article in a paper or magazine.

In spite of this dearth of written knowledge, practical men in all parts of the world were rapidly improving the methods of treatment, both mechanically and with the aid of chemistry, in their several localities; but, through lack of exchange of thought, each section had a different process, on which faith was pinned to the exclusion of all other processes.

As the rich deposits gave out, attention was turned to those of lower grade, which are now found to be very profitable with improved machinery and increased knowledge, but, even to-day, we are in the infancy of this science. The treatises on gold, now before the public, can still be counted on the fingers of one hand, and are either devoted to the scientific discussions of processes now in vogue, the history past and present of gold milling, or the mechanics pure and simple of the various machinery used. They are all good for the education of the world, but are lacking in definite directions of the best way to employ the methods they describe, and are generally understood by those only who have enjoyed a previous technical education. This absence of intelligent application of these known principles in the great majority of the mills in this State (the home of gold milling), has been a constant source of wonder to me, and yet I have a fellow feeling from my first experiences in gold-mill practice. Graduating from a celebrated school of mining engineering, I thought myself eminently fit to at once assume the absolute management of the biggest mining concern on earth, but, thanks to the kind influence of an elder brother, already well known in the mining world, I was started at the bottom of the ladder in a gold mill, to begin my real education. I very soon found that there was no bigger tenderfoot in California, as my technical education had only taught the chemistry and scientific mechanics in general, with no practical rules of how to apply this knowledge. These practical rules have been learned through bitter experience, extending through many years, and to try and help others who are just beginning, I have set down in the following pages the results of the observations I have made, all of which have been practically demonstrated as correct by application on several very difficult ores, with marked success in every case. It has been a work of pleasure to contribute this mite of knowledge, and if I am instrumental in increasing the production of only one gold mill, I will feel amply repaid for my labor.

I ask the indulgence of the reader, to overlook the absence of rounded sentences and polished language, and take the will for the deed. I have done the best I am able, and can only leave the verdict to the public.

W. J. ADAMS, E. M.

San Francisco.

CHAPTER I.

GENERAL PROCESS.

It is not the purpose, in this book, to enter into any detailed description of "gold milling," as the ground has already been amply covered by E. B. Preston, in his report on "Gold Milling," published by the "State Mineralogist," of California.

Some other points also may seem too well known and appreciated to be mentioned, but these require constant repetition, and even then very little practical application seems to be made by the average millman.

In order clearly to understand the entire method, we must start with the ore as it comes from the mine. This ore must first be carefully examined, as its character and structure as well as its value, determine the most advantageous method to pursue. First, the ore may be hard and tough, requiring force to disintegrate it, though entirely free-milling; second, the ore may be soft, giving a great deal of slimes; third, the ore may be a mixture of the above two divisions.

First: Here, the ore is first dumped over a grizzly, with the bars set 1½ inch apart, the coarse lumps going through a rock-breaker of some form, to mix with the fines in the ore bin. From this bin it must be carried to stamps, preferably of heavy weight, notwithstanding all assertions to the contrary by patentees and makers of other pulverizing devices which are "just as good as stamps."

Second· When the ore is soft, it also requires to be passed through a breaker, to enable the particles to be of uniform size; but here, very frequently any kind of stamp, and always those of heavy weight, will slush through the bed of pulp, wearing out iron uselessly, and increase the proportion of slimes, always to be avoided as much as possible. Here we find a great advantage in the different types of the Chilian mill, such as the Huntington and Bryan, from both of which the pulp escapes as soon as it is reduced to the requisite size, as determined by the screen, and with the minimum of slimes to hinder future operations.

Third: In an ore containing both soft, clayey or talcose material, and hard bunches of quartz, stamps are generally the best, as the grit of the hard quartz prevents pounding of iron on iron, and causes sufficient splash to keep the screens from choking, while all operations can be kept under close observation, which cannot be done with any pan or roller mill—one of the greatest objections to the general use of these mills. In some few cases, however, where the output from the mine is sufficiently large to warrant the outlay of capital, it will be found of great benefit to separate the ore partially and automatically into two classes. Dumping the ore over a long grizzly, the soft and fine will go into one bin, while the coarse, after being put through the breaker, falls into a second bin. That from the first bin is fed to one or more roller-pan mills, while the hard broken quartz goes to the stamp mill, very largely increasing in this way the output through the two methods combined.

The pulverized ore, technically known as "battery pulp," is now carried by water down silver-plated copper plates, by which means as much of the gold as possible is abstracted, varying very considerably under different millmen's methods; a low percentage saved, being excused by such terms as "floured gold," that floats in water, rusty gold, "plumbago in the ore," or a similar state of affairs.

However, there is generally sufficient gold left in this pulp, which could never be saved with quicksilver, to require further treatment, while the value is too low to treat all the pulp en masse. This gold is either, mechanically or chemically, locked up with other metalliferous substances, generally sulphides or minerals of a higher specific gravity than the accompanying gangue.

This specific gravity is the keystone to all the concentrating devices, and the special method required is determined by only two facts, the value of the concentrates when pure, and the percentage of them carried by the ore. Should these concentrates be of low value and moderately coarse, a simple bumping table, like the Gilpin County bumping table, or its improvement, the Wilfley, could be used, as they require little care, are reasonable in price, and save concentrates free from foreign matter, while the final tailings, though still carrying a large percentage of mineral, will be economically valueless owing to the intrinsically low value of the sulphurets. When, however, the concentrates are of value, for instance above $50 per ton, a mechanism of much greater delicacy must be employed, and of all the devices, none has proved so satisfactory as an endless moving belt, shaking without a jar. As a rule, the higher the grade of sulphurets the more friable they are, and the finest slimes, most easily affected by agitation, carry the richest particles, reaching a culmination in the tellurides. Should the "battery pulp" carry a high percentage of **sulphurets**, that is, above 12 per **cent.**, **it** very often becomes **necessary** to use a double concentration, and in **this case two** machines of the same **type** are used, the tailings from the first passing directly to the second, after removing the surplus water if there is too much added on the first machine.

In spite of all these precautions, it is very frequently found that the concentrator tailings still carry an appreciable value, and most thorough tests must be made to determine whether or not this can be economically saved. The first and commonest method is to allow the tailings to run over a large surface, covered with canvas, which is cleaned and swept several times a day, but, generally, this only saves a small percentage of the loss, and its only advantage is its cheapness. With proper care and experience the concentrators should save all that the canvas plant could do, and any further reduction must treat economically with the entire mass.

So far the only way to do this is by employing some of the modifications of the "cyanide process," and this requires a large tank capacity, so that the tailings can flow directly to the filtering tanks.

This is concisely the method of gold milling, but there are several points to observe, to insure complete success on the majority of ores.

First, foremost and at all times is the question of grease. Guard against its excessive use day and night, month and year. Keep all the bearings and machinery where it is used as scrupulously clean as a New England housewife does her home; do not grudge the use of clean waste, but see that the employees observe the maximum of cleanliness. Bits of candles do no harm, or very little, if made of stearic acid, but beware of tallow dips. Start in with the rock breaker, and place dripping pans underneath the journals, making frequent examinations to see that all the drops are caught. See that none of the oil used on the running gear of the self-feeders drops on the feeder floor, being very careful about working the leakage of ore always found underneath the feeders, if there is the slightest possibility of its being fouled. Clean the stems of the stamps, the cams and tappets very frequently, and do not use liquid oil on them, but make a swab of blanket and apply a minimum of axle grease, to the cams several times a day, to the stems only as needed. When applied to the stems, only touch them above the guides. It is generally better to tack some canvas between the camshaft floor and the top of the lower guides, giving to it a decided belly, to prevent any grease thrown by the cams from falling into the feeder or throat of mortar, or on the plates. In one mill, where very poor work had been done, though the builder and superintendent claimed most thorough knowledge, we found boards placed below the cams to prevent the grease from falling on the plates, and set at such an angle that there was a constant rolling of pellets of grease directly into the throat of the mortar.

We now come to the concentrators, and it can be safely stated, with hardly an exception, that the cleanliness of the machines is a sure indication of the quality of work done, and the closeness of saving accomplished.

Where rubber belts are used, the oil rots them, the sand and grit get into the bearings, causing bumping, inequality of the plane of the table, and a little grease getting into the pulp will prevent the saving of the finest and richest of the sulphurets. The very act of cleaning the machines brings all parts under close scrutiny, and many a serious break-down is averted, observed in time during this cleaning at regular intervals. Therefore, be sure and watch for grease, daily caution the employes about it, spare no pains nor expense to have every part

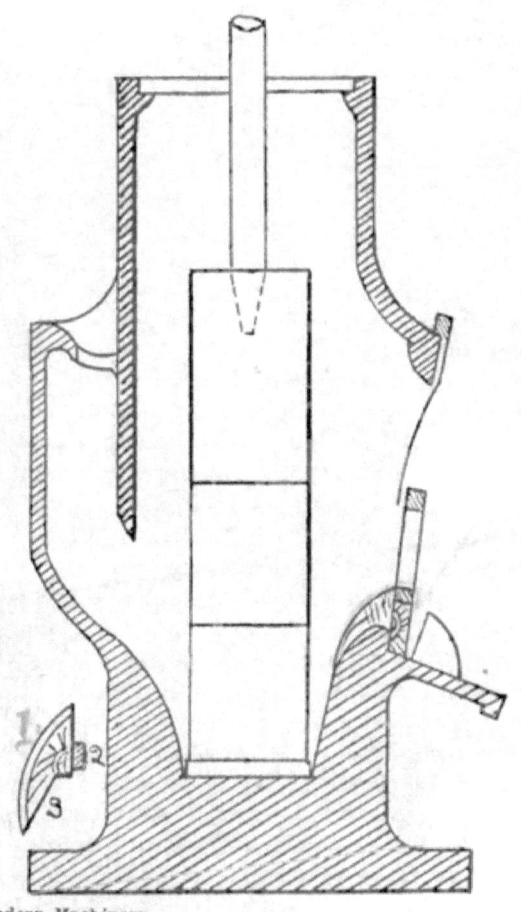

Modern Machinery.

FIG. 1.
1—Copper plate. 2—Iron strip. 3—Wood backing.

of the **mill at** all times as if on parade, and the close saving **and** freedom from break-downs will amply repay all the trouble and outlay.

Within certain limits the shape of the mortar does not **affect the** economic results nearly as much as has been supposed—that depending mostly on the man attending to them. A mortar must be narrow, as the object is to get the ore out of the battery as fast as crushed. The back should be curved from the throat, so **as to** throw the ore directly on the center of the "die." **This** back must be solid metal, and on **no** account have copper plates in the back. Their advantage is very dubious, and in nine cases out of ten their **use** is a very great detriment to successful work. Without them the copper plates on the "chuck-blocks" catch as much amalgam **as** both combined; there is less surface to scour, particularly with low-grade ore, and with them the additional **width** of the mortar prevents the splash being exerted exclusively against the screen, and reduces the crushing capacity of the battery. (See Fig. 1.)

The discharge, that is, the distance between the top of die and bottom of screen, should be within a fraction of four inches, new dies requiring wooden strips under the screens to keep this height. The "drop" **of** the stamps should be $4\frac{1}{2}$ to 5 inches, and the speed always above 95 drops per minute, preferably above 100 drops. A slow drop, besides decreasing the duty of the stamps, allows the quicksilver to settle and diminishes its comminution so that too much is liable to be used at one time, a sure loss if the gold is floured. A quick, short drop more nearly approaches the action of the pan in **pan** amalgamation, keeping all the pulp in constant **agitation, and** mixing the quicksilver uniformly, so that **all parts of the** ore come in contact with it before leaving **the battery.**

The "chuck-block," covered with the copper plate, should be entirely separated from the strip of wood on which the screen rests. The plate should touch the bottom of the screen itself, at as slight an angle as possible, and should be very nearly vertical and five inches deep. Its backing, generally of wood, must be as slight as possible, so as to place it far from the dies. It is held

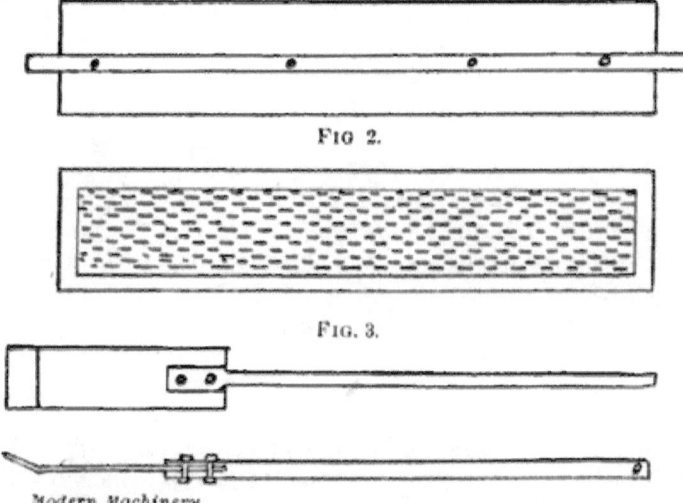

Fig 2.

Fig. 3.

Modern Machinery.   Fig. 4.

in place by a strip of iron, which extends into the shoulders on each side of the mortar.

Two chuck-blocks should be made with the blocks to conform to the **height** of the screen as the dies wear down, as with **dies** half worn the wooden strip underneath the screen is removed, bringing the discharge **down** to normal height, and the copper must not project above the bottom of the screen-discharge.

This sketch, made without a scale, as the width of mortars varies, will better explain it. Figure 2 shows both cross-section and longitudinal section.

The screens (see Fig. 3) are preferably made with openings eight inches high, and the entire length of the mortar. Abstain from putting any cross-pieces, which obstruct the freedom of discharge. In placing the screens the chuck-block is first put in place, then the strip of wood on which the screen rests, having a lining of blanket tacked to both edges, and this strip of wood is keyed by the shoulders cast on the lip of the mortar. Then the screen is put in place and keyed by the wedges driven down the shoulders on each side of mortar. There still remains a large opening between the top of screen and the bottom of the upper casting of the mortar itself. This should be wide enough, even with new dies, to allow of the easy insertion of the arm to the shoulder. In most mills this is very foolishly closed solidly by a wooden false screen and keyed as tightly as the screen itself. The proper way is to take a strip of wood the full outside width of the mortar in length, and 2x1 inches, and on this tack very strongly either extra-heavy canvas or a piece of rubber belting, which just fills the opening in width and extends a little below the upper edge of screen-frame, in depth. The advantages of this should be obvious, but a few of them may be named: First, it permits the inspection of the interior of the battery at all times, without stopping the stamps; second, the cleaning, twice daily, of all accumulated chips and other clogging of the inside of screen; third, the examination by touch of the amalgam accumulating on chuck-block; and, fourth, in many cases, the driving on and replacing of shoes without removing the screen.

The greatest advantage of all is that the mill is stopped as little as possible, and hence the most perfect amalgamation maintained, while no hard amalgam is broken away, as always occurs when the screen is removed. In fact, as my first great point was "avoid grease," my second is, "Never remove the screen of a battery till the run is ended, if it can possibly be avoided, and the finer the gold the more important this is."

It takes a very appreciable time, after a battery is started, no matter how short the stop may be, before all the pulp is in constant agitation, and the quicksilver mixed with it.

This rule also brings us to the proper material of which to have the screens made, and in this as well as everything else, the best is always the cheapest. Theoretically, wire screens expose the most discharging surface, but they clog the quickest, and have to be removed to be cleaned by a wire brush, a very serious fault, as stated above. Round-punched holes present too much dead surface, being exactly the reverse of the wire screens. This only leaves us the "burr-slot" and the "punched-slot," and of these the burr-slot, though clogging the least of any, wears coarser more quickly than the punched-slot. Therefore the advice we give is to use in stamp batteries "punched-slot screens," of the best material to be had. Of material we have tinplate, Russia iron and steel. Tinplate is the cheapest, but the screens are worn out within a few days, and are really the most expensive in the results that can possibly be employed. Russia iron will not break easily, but the orifices wear so coarse within 48 hours, particularly on hard quartz, that the ore will not be pulverized as fine as required. This leaves us only the steel, which breaks before it wears coarse, on account of its hardness. Of course there is steel and steel, but if a point is made about it, steel screens can be procured which will not break for over a month under rough usage, and even in that time the size of the apertures has not appreciably increased, i. e., sufficiently to cause any loss in free gold.

Here we have the best condition, the battery in steady operation for a month, the pulp in steady and constant agitation, no disturbance of the hard amalgam, by removing a screen; and the greater the quantity of amalgam in the battery, the more of the fine and floured gold is caught there. Therefore use a "steel, punched-slot screen," of the size found by experiment to be the best. Several factors determine this size.

With coarse gold this is not of so much moment, but should the gold be fine, it is necessary to crack the ore that much more to free it. This degree of pulverizing depends on the grade of the ore, as in many cases it costs more to save the finest gold than the total amount saved, and it then becomes necessary in practical reduction to use a larger sized screen, put through more rock, and pay little attention to additional loss in the tailings. However, it is best to use as fine a screen as is conformable with a profit in working the mine.

The outside of the screen must be scraped several times a day, and as good a device as any is a copper spade with the edge turned over at an angle of 45 degrees; wooden handle, copper riveted, as shown in Fig. 4.

There should be a long expanse of copper-plate surface below each battery, though some of it is only of use in case of faulty amalgamation.

These plates are technically divided into:

INSIDE COPPER CHUCK-BLOCK, a description of which has already been given, and there is only to add that it is an unnecessary expense to have it silver-plated.

LIP-PLATE, which must be heavily silvered, at least three ounces of silver to the square foot being put on it.

This plate is just the length of the mortar and is wide enough to extend from the inside-edge against which the bottom of screen is braced, to a half-inch beyond the iron lip of mortar. Two rectangular holes are cut in it, to allow the shoulders of lower keys to project, and the wooden strip on which the screen rests is placed on top of the plate and holds it solidly in position.

SPLASH PLATE.—This is rarely found, even in the

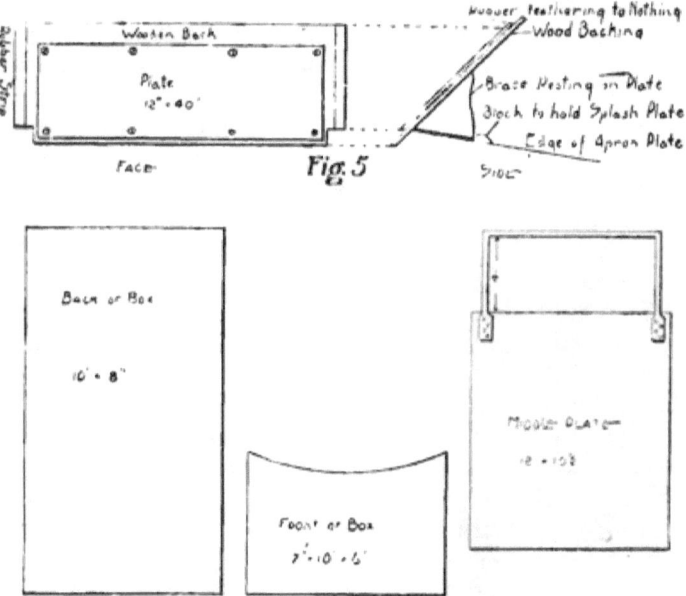

best mills, but is of the utmost importance; the more so, as the gold is floured. In fact, it is absolutely necessary if very fine gold is to be saved. It should be 12 inches wide, by a length just sufficient to fill the space between the shoulders of the mortar. There are several ways of adjusting, but in every one the point to be observed is, that it shall stand in front of the screens at an angle never less than forty-five degrees and better if over fifty degrees from horizontal; that the bottom shall be at least an inch below the bottom of the screen, and the space between the screen-frame and it shall not exceed three-quarters of an inch. Take this plate and fasten it to an inch board, leaving a margin of the board below the copper plate, to act as a brace to the stalactites slowly formed, and then by back supports, stand it on the edge of the next plates, so that it is held firmly against the mortar and yet can be instantly removed, as shown in Fig. 5.

Another way of great simplicity, which, however, has the objection of causing too much jar, is to rivet a piece of track iron on each shoulder, at the angle the plate shall stand, and slide the plate down, keeping it away from the screen by a false strip tacked to the front of the board, along each side of the plate itself.

By studying the effect of this its advantages can easily be seen. Twenty years ago it was universal to have a spray of clear water constantly dropping on the apron-plate to form a slight stoppage of the pulp and cause the amalgamated gold to settle and attach itself to the plate, but, as future working of the pulp was very much hindered by this excess of water, it is now rarely used. Again, to a certain extent, the output of the mill is increased the greater the amount of water allowed to flow into the battery, and as a result, all the water that could be used and not hinder future operations, is allowed to run into the mortars.

No matter how fine the gold may be, if it is free, under proper amalgamation, it will adhere to an amalgamated surface if brought into actual contact with it, and this the splash-plate does in two ways. First, half of the pulp is thrown against it in a coarse spray, aiding adhesion by the force; second, it then runs down the plate, dropping off the bottom exactly similar to the spray from the clear water troughs used in earlier times, forming a dam and eddies, which cause the other half of the pulp to precipitate its fine amalgam at this point.

From here, the object to be attained is to have no rapid and strong currents. To turn the pulp over and over, so that all parts are frequently brought in contact with the amalgamated surface, and to spread this pulp as thin as consistent with keeping it in constant motion and allowing no settling of even the heavy sulphurets on the plates. It is also found that an occasional drop of one inch to one and one-half inches is a benefit.

Now we come to one of the greatest mistakes made by 90 per cent. of all amalgamators, an error held to like the grip of death by men of broad technical education, causing the failure of many properties which should be successful.

This is the grade given to the large plates. These should never be placed with less than 2½ inches to each foot, and in most cases 3 inches would be better, and even more, while better work can be done at an angle of forty-five degrees than with a grade less than 2½ inches.

Take a case where the plates are set below 2½ inches, we find an excess of water required to keep all the pulp moving and, therefore, too great a depth, so that the fine gold is held in solution and never touches the amalgamated surface, when we truly have float gold, while an equally bad feature, almost universal, is that it allows too much quicksilver to be used, and fine gold will never be saved with even a slight excess of quicksilver. This point will be more fully explained under the discussion of amalgamation.

HINTS ON AMALGAMATION.

With the plates at the proper grade and the requisite amount of water, the pulp travels down the plates in a succession of waves, the lower edge of each wave rolling over and over and bringing every particle of water even, in contact several times with the amalgamated surface. The more sulphides the ore carries, the steeper must be the grade of the plates, to clear them and still not interfere with the concentration of the tailings.

After this explanation we can continue the description of the plates.

From the lip-plate the pulp has a drop of nearly two inches and falls on the first plate separate from the mortar.

The apron-plate should be divided into two sections, the first easily removed at all times. This should be the full length of the mortar, and two feet wide, and that end nearest the battery resting on the wooden shelf fastened to wooden mortar-block, and held in place by the lip of the mortar or a strong hook on each side, while the lower end rests on the second section. This second section must have the same width, and be from 4 to 6 feet long. It is supported by extension legs firmly secured to the floor. By using this form of support the grade of the table can be changed to suit the ore, after practical experiment. Start with a grade of $2\frac{1}{2}$ to 3 inches, and, if too much water is required to keep all the pulp in steady motion, lower the second section (the first assuming the same grade, as it rests on it), until the pulp is seen to move freely and in successive waves with a minimum of water.

On most ores this amount of plate surface is all that is necessary, but if there is still sufficient fall to allow the tailings to be readily carried away automatically, the pulp is now passed over "sluice plates," as a safeguard against accidents, after passing through a quicksilver trap.

These sluice plates are 18 inches wide and from 8 to 10 feet long, and are set at a minimum angle of 1⅞ inch per foot. All the plates should have a coating of silver of three ounces to every square foot, although on the sluice plates two ounces will do.

There are several devices for traps, but most of them are only receptacles where a slight obstruction to the flow of the current is given and this is not enough. We want to accomplish two objects: first, retain all the amalgam and quicksilver that may have escaped the copper plates; second, secure this with a minimum of sand and sulphurets.

A large open box is always filled with sand which is gradually replaced by coarser sand and sulphurets according to the length of time before its complete removal, while only a modicum of loss is arrested here. The next result of experimenting caused the pulp to descend on one side and rise on the other of a partition, the higher specific gravity of the valuable portions aiding their retention, and it is on this principle, that the most successful traps are now constructed; the best of all being those used in the mills of the "Homestake" in the Black Hills, and designated as the "Black Hills Trap."

This can easily be constructed of wood by any good carpenter, as it consists of a wooden box with sheet iron partitions, loosely set in grooves cut in the sides of the box. A trap for five stamps is given here. It is made of 1½ inch clear lumber; inside measure horizontally 10 inches wide by 8 inches; depth at inlet, 18 inches; at outlet, 6 inches. Plough three grooves equally distant in each side and ¼ inch deep, making them

HINTS ON AMALGAMATION.   27

wide enough to allow a sheet of heavy iron or copper to slide readily up and down. The middle groove should extend clear to the bottom of box while the other two are stopped 2 inches from the bottom.

Fig. 6 shows the details of construction of box, a perspective view and the method of attaching handle to the middle partition.

The first iron or copper plate is cut 10½ inches wide and 18 inches long, with a handle riveted to its upper

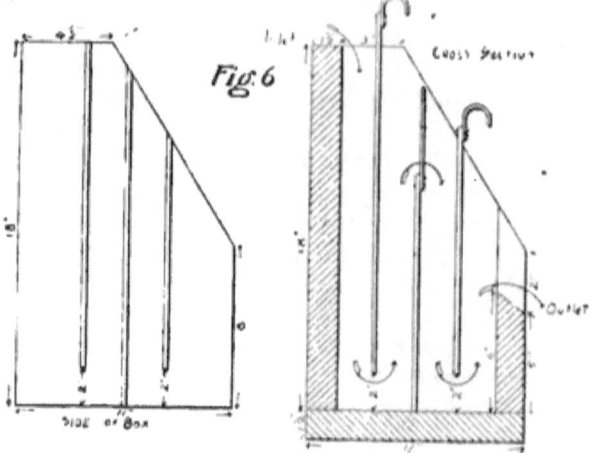

edge. The second is cut 10½ inches wide and 12 inches long, with a rod riveted at each side and extending up 4 inches, as shown in cut. The third is like the second, 10½x12 inches, with a handle riveted on its upper edge like the first.

Here we have at two separate times 6 inches' pressure to force the pulp, the first time a vertical distance of 12 inches, the second time a distance of 6 inches, both practically prohibiting the escape of a metal of such a

28   HINTS ON AMALGAMATION.

high specific gravity as quicksilver, even if very finely
comminuted and still not enough to prevent the escape
of all the pulp and sulphurets except a slight layer less
than two inches, which also is in constant agitation as

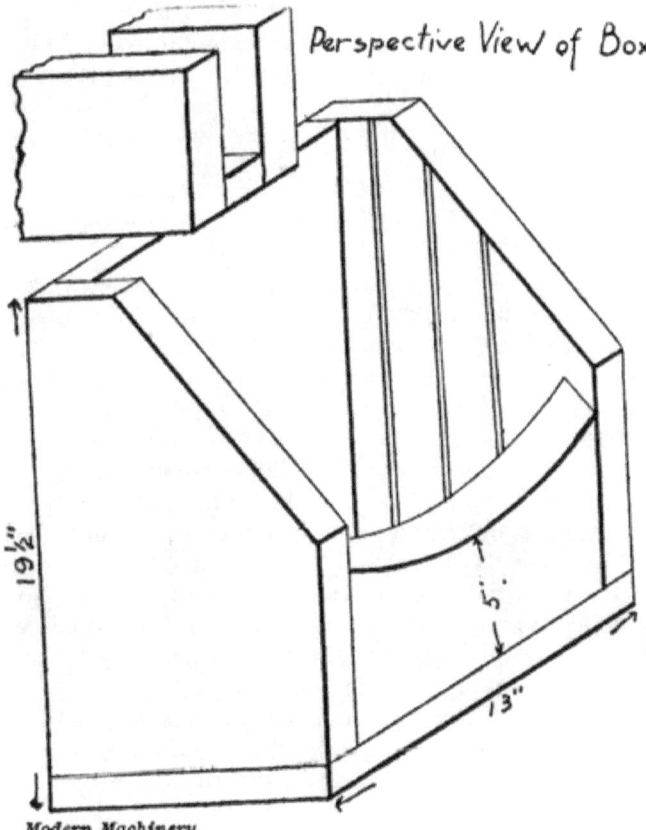
Modern Machinery.

long as the same amount of water is employed. Should
this water get slack from any cause, the first division
at once becomes choked, but the trap is quickly freed

HINTS ON AMALGAMATION.

by raising the first partition. When the trap is cleaned all the partitions are withdrawn and the residue, very small in quantity, is removed.

The pulp, on leaving the apron-plate, falls into a box with the bottom sloping from each side to a central vent, from which it flows directly into the trap, and on leaving the trap, either flows over the sluice-plates, or,

Modern Machinery.

in their absence, into wooden or iron launders, to be conveyed to the concentrators. Fig. 7 shows two cross-sections of the box in front of apron-plates.

The battery tailings, after leaving the sluice-plates, or, if they are absent, the amalgam trap, fall directly into the concentrating launders. These are preferably made of wood, as iron pipes, if choked by broom straws, pieces of blanket, etc., have to be disjointed to be cleaned. These wooden boxes, troughs or launders measure inside 4 inches wide by 6 inches high, and must have at the very least a grade of ⅞ inch per running foot. Now, under the most careful management, a little amalgam and quicksilver escapes all the devices mentioned above, and it is advisable to put in a couple of "riffles" in each box length of 12 feet. This is done in this way: Before the bottom piece is nailed to the sides, make a saw-cut at right angles to the length equally distant and a half inch deep, and then gouge out to it from the upper side. This is shown in Fig. 8.

If the water used is always the same in quantity, a V-shaped box will carry the sand with the smallest amount, but should the water slacken at all the sand at once makes a broader surface and then from the increased friction and breadth the launder is at once filled to the top. To gain some advantage from the V-shaped form we have found great benefit in putting angle strips

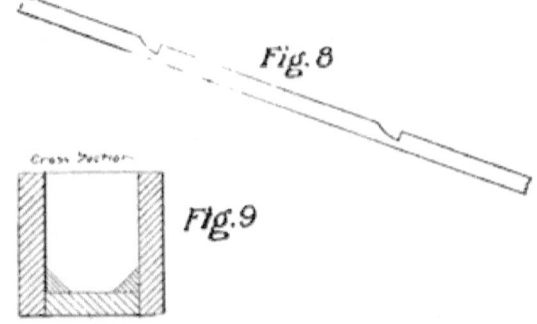

Modern Machinery.

along each side of the box, 1 inch wide and 1 inch high, giving a 2 inch bottom with flaring sides, as shown in Fig. 9.

When the pulp is divided over two machines a division with a long swinging finger is put in and each launder reduced to a width of 2 inches, from the end of which it is carried by a rubber hose to the concentrators.

THE CONCENTRATORS.—As stated in the beginning, all sulphurets of a value above $50 per ton require a shaking table with an endless belt that must work without a jar, and be at all times completely under the control of the operator.

Two classes of machines are in vogue, one shaking sidewise or across the stream, the other with an end-shake against and with the stream. Years of practical experience have proved that the end-shake concentrators cannot produce concentrates free from foreign matter, though in some cases the tailings have a very low valuation, while any attempt to make clean headings results in excessive loss. This can readily be seen as the upstroke against the current exerts too great a force against the clear water regulated for the downstroke, while if regulated with sufficient force to keep the sand back on the upstroke, it washes down the finer and lighter sulphurets during the downstroke. This has been acknowledged by the inventors of the end-shake machines, from the fact of the universal application of the side-shake since that special patent has expired.

The first of these side-shake machines is still taken as the standard, being superior in the estimation of the world in its operation and ease of adjustment, and far ahead in the quality of material employed in its construction. This makes it, however, the most expensive at first cost, though the cheapest in the end. This is known as the "Frue Vanner," and the general application of all being the same, it will be taken to illustrate the general method of concentration. However, we wish first to explain the reason for the use of a wooden frame, to which some objection is made. It is this, that there is sufficient spring to a wooden frame to prevent any jar to the table as it is thrown an inch each way, and this jar is always very perceptible on all the machines resting on a rigid iron frame.

We will now continue the course of the battery tailings. The concentrator is set with a grade regulated by screws at the foot, up which and against the current the endless belt travels, and this grade is arranged so that there is at all times a thickness of pulp of ½ inch which is neither stiff nor sticky. The speed of the shaking motion for average ores is started at 190 revolutions per minute, and then the proper grade is determined only after actual experiment. The pulp falls on the machine near its upper end, being uniformly distributed by the "ore-spreader" over the entire width of the belt. On this ore-spreader it is well to have a silver-plated copper plate, as this is the last opportunity to catch separately any amalgam or quicksilver that may have escaped all the other devices.

The ore-spreader must deliver the pulp to the belt with as little splash as possible so as not to disturb the sulphurets that have already settled. To do this there should be a step added, as shown in Fig. 10, to break the fall, and this step must just clear the surface of the pulp already on the machine.

In front of this ore-spreader is placed a clear water distributer, which supplies just enough water to separate the remnants of sand from the sulphurets, and take the place of the water coming down with the pulp. The water should be just enough to keep all the field between the water distributor and the ore-spreader covered with water without a current. Too little water is shown by a series of dry fingers against which the finest sulphurets shake, become dry and float down the machine uncaught. Should some sand come up with the sulphurets and no dry fingers be exposed, do not turn on more water, but either decrease the speed of the uphill travel of the belt if the bed of pulp is the right depth and not sticky, or give the machine a steeper grade by lowering the foot. The tailings from the concentrators under proper management should show by panning tests no more sulphurets, though perhaps an assay by fire will still show that too much is being lost, either in sulphurets too finely slimed to be collected by hand tests or in tellurides, oxidized minerals or carbonates. Very often these fine slimes can be saved with coarse canvas,

HINTS ON AMALGAMATION.

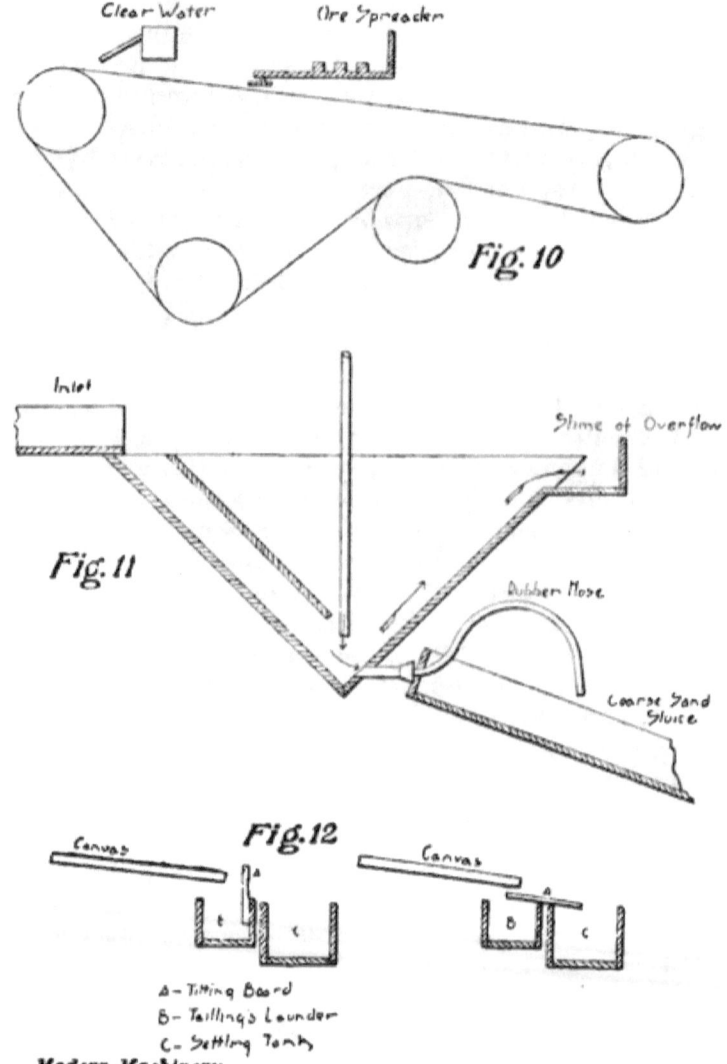

Fig. 10

Fig. 11

Fig. 12

A — Tilting Board
B — Tailings Launder
C — Settling Tank

Modern Machinery.

requiring very little additional expense except the first outlay in erecting the plant. We can safely say that in ninety-nine per cent. of these cases all the value is in the slimes, so that our first duty is a mechanical separation or sizing. This separating is done with the well-known "spitz-kasten," a V-shaped box divided by a partition. Here the coarse sand is drawn out through a hole at the point of the V, while the slimes overflow at the top, clear water being added to help the separation. The cross-section in Fig. 11 will explain the principle.

The slimes and water are now carried in launders to the canvas plates, always made in duplicate to allow the cleaning of one set while the slimes are flowing over the other. The cleaning is done with a broom and in some cases a spray of clear water under pressure. The tables are made of matched lumber, varying from 4 feet to 12 feet wide and 10 feet long. They are set at a grade of 1½ inches for each running foot, and are covered with No. 6 canvas. As stated above, the tables must either be made in duplicate or, in a large plant, a couple of extra tables are provided, to be used while cleaning those in steady use. The slimes and water flow down one series of tables for a definite time, generally one to three hours, when the pulp is turned off and a small amount of clear water is used to carry off a little of the waste. Then a tilting board is placed under the foot of the table and the concentrates swept and washed into the settling box. The concentrates, if rich enough, are shipped without further handling, but it is found occasionally to be of benefit to reconcentrate them over a machine set with very little grade, and running at a very low speed. We show in Fig. 12 the method of saving the washings of the canvas plates, as generally adopted in California.

CHAPTER II.

CARE OF QUICKSILVER.

It is generally acknowledged that special care must be exercised to keep the quicksilver absolutely pure and lively, and the advice given is to retort it, as that will eliminate all the impurities. This is a fallacy, because there are certain elements which will vaporize with the quicksilver and still contaminate it, so that even after retorting we find it necessary to resort to chemical agencies to establish its highest efficiency. We buy a flask of quicksilver from the producers, and generally find it absolutely pure, but at times the mass will separate into globules which have a repellent power, one on the other. This is probably caused from the use of lime in the retorting of metal from its ore of cinnabar. Lime has a peculiar effect on quicksilver, as a slight addition to sluggish metal, separated into globules will not only liven it up but cause the globules to join together, while an excess will increase more than fourfold the repellance of the globules toward each other. Therefore, we must suppose the fresh unused quicksilver is contaminated by too much lime. Two chemicals are open to our use, both of which will destroy, pound for pound, an equal amount of the quicksilver, viz., a strong solution of cyanide of potassium, or a weak one of nitric acid. Now, nitric acid causes fuming, and renders the millman susceptible to salivation, so that it is better to use cyanide, if possible, in all our operations of cleansing.

When the practical adaptation of the solubility of gold in cyanide of potassium became generally known, the majority of millmen, and more especially the owners of mines, were afraid to use any cyanide in their operations, as they believed they were liable to lose much of the fine gold in the ore, dissolved by the cyanide. This is a very erroneous impression, except in a case where cyanide in solution was mixed with the ore previous to the introduction of quicksilver. In other words, cyanide of potassium has the greatest affinity for grease and copper, and will also dissolve quicksilver, if present, without affecting the gold at all. This enables us to use this chemical in conjunction with quicksilver to great advantage in all our operations. Always, then, before using any of the quicksilver, add to it a solution of cyanide, and a strong solution is better than a weak one; in fact, we have used a saturated solution with benefit. Some of the quicksilver is poured into a china bowl and the surface is covered at least to a depth of one-half inch with the solution, with which it must always be kept covered. As each spoonful of quicksilver is fed into the batteries it is thoroughly brightened and cleansed in passing through the supernatant liquid, and is in the best condition to catch the gold. After the quicksilver has been in use in the mill, it is frequently spoiled by certain elements in the ore, or some accidental fouling, such as the heating of a journal and the consequent flowing of babbit metal into the ore-bin. From the elements in the ore, we find lead, tellurium, and selenium. The worst fouling, however, comes from babbit metal. This turns the quicksilver black, making it slimy and frothy. In this case retorting of the quantity contaminated must be resorted to, but a partial help can be had by using sulhpuric acid, allowing the

HINTS ON AMALGAMATION.

fuming to go on for several hours, with occasional stirring. The loss is very great. Should the ore contain tellurium or selenium, it will always be found necessary to purify the quicksilver after retorting, as these metals are carried over with the quicksilver in distilling the quicksilver from the amalgam. Here we must employ nitric acid, allowing it to fume for several hours. Then, after washing thoroughly, a solution of cyanide is added, turning the liquid black. On removing this with a sponge, the quicksilver is found to be in perfect condition. Some advise the addition of a small amount of sodium amalgam to the quicksilver, but personally we are very averse to using it on account of its causing even the iron of the mortar to be amalgamated, while the amalgam on the plates is kept too soft.

Turning then to the room especially set apart for chemicals and quicksilver, and specifically known as the clean-up room, we need to keep in stock all our supplies, which consist of the following list: Commercial cyanide of potassium, C. P. nitric acid, C. P. Sulpuhic acid, 10 pounds of copperas or sulphate of iron, 10 pounds of blue-stone or sulphate of copper, some pieces of soft chalk for lining the retort, a heavy horseshoe magnet, a 40-mesh screen 18 inches in diameter for sieving wood-ashes, a mortar and pestle of one quart capacity and one of two quarts, two gold pans and one copper bottom pan, two white enameled iron pails, two porcelain lined kettles with bales, of one gallon capacity and two of half gallon, several pint and quart stoneware bowls, and several cups without handles, a large carriage sponge and several smaller sponges, a few yards of fine canvas, one-half dozen whisk brooms of better quality than the ordinary clothes brushes, a couple of scrubbing brushes, one-half dozen hand whitewash brushes, a

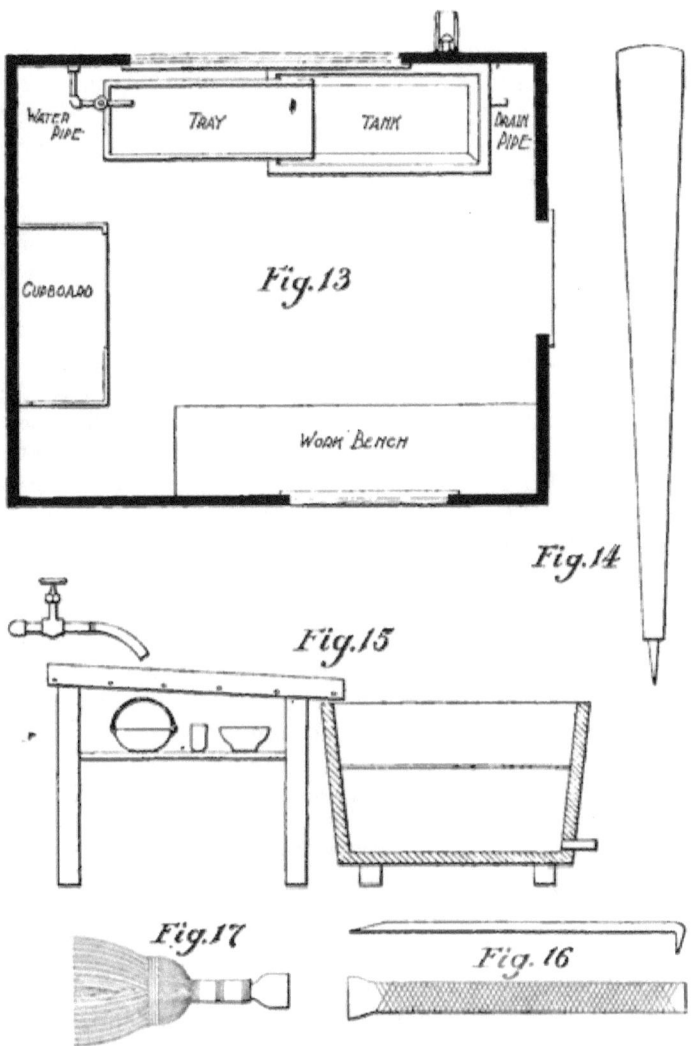

Modern Machinery.

HINTS ON AMALGAMATION.

couple of square rubber scrapers, or, what is better, new rubber belting with sharply cut edges, having at least a dozen already prepared, and a small platform scale for weighing the quicksilver and amalgam. This should use avordupois weights, as it is only the bullion itself that is weighed in troy ounces.

Make the floor of matched lumber, on top of the regular flooring, with a tightly fitted baseboard all around the room, remembering that quicksilver is very elusive and disappears from no apparent cause. This room is placed to one side of the battery floor with one window that commands a full view of the batteries on one side, and a window letting in light from the outside, directly in front of the clean-up tank, while the door, secured by a padlock, leads from inside the mill and never from the outside, so that all persons before getting to this important room must pass before the observation of the mill employees. A ground plan is given in Fig. 13.

The work-bench is made of 2-inch lumber, with solid legs that will not jar the room when heavy hammering is done. On this old screens are removed from their frames and new ones put on, and as there is always some amalgam attached to the old screens, the top of the table must be tight so that the residue can be collected and planned. The implements required, each of which should have its place just above the table, are, a light hammer, a steel scraper (home made, either from an old file or a putty knife), a tack extractor, a pair of snips or tin shears, and a punch to enable the tacks to enter the steel. The only tacks of any account are those known as upholstery, ordinary carpet tacks invariably losing their heads, while small wire nails are held too firmly by the wood for subsequent withdrawal on replacing the screens. The punch is made of steel, similar to a scratch-awl, or according to Fig. 14. There must also be here, ready to hand, a piece of blanket of good quality and strips of wood of various sizes, for patching a hole in a screen temporarily, when it is not advisable to remove it just then, as, for instance, during the night when nearing the end of a run, with so much amalgam inside the battery that, to save any further dispute, it will be as well only to open the battery in the presence of the party who is directly responsible. A stock of screen frames with new screens on and ready for use must always be kept on hand, and this reserve should never be less than three, as in no instance is the old adage so exemplified of "time being money" than the moments lost in stopping a battery from its work. In putting the new screens on the frame, be sure that the rough side, presenting the smallest openings is on the inside.

The cupboard must be arranged to be kept under lock and key, be fitted with shelves on which all the supplies, scrapers, chemicals, assortment of wire nails and quicksilver are kept, but no oil or grease must be allowed in this room.

In arranging the tray and panning tank, we must get the best light possible on our work, and therefore they must be placed in front of the window on the outside of the building. The tank must be 4 feet 6 inches by 2 feet on top and tapering to the bottom, where the dimensions are 4 feet by 18 inches. It must be 2 feet 6 inches deep. Six inches from the top is placed an overflow pipe, discharging outside the building into a sluice a few inches wide, either set with riffles or covered with a copper plate, while a drain hole, stopped with a plug, is bored just above the bottom. A slat is tacked along

HINTS ON AMALGAMATION.

each side, a foot from the top, on which a movable wooden grate can be placed, to rest a pan while breaking up the lumps, or a screen that requires washing.

On the left side, and projecting an inch over the tank, is placed the tray solidly built and absolutely water-tight. This should be 4 feet 6 inches long, and at least 18 inches wide, have a bottom preferably of one piece of 1½-inch clear lumber, having edgings 2 inches high on three sides, and open in front of the tank with a gutter along this open side to collect any quicksilver that may run down. The slope should be ½-inch to each foot. Over this tray must be placed a clear-water pipe, ½ or ¾-inch, fitted with a globe valve and a piece of rubber hose 12 to 18 inches long. This is explained in the sketch of Fig. 15.

On this tray the chuck blocks are scraped and all the amalgam put through its final cleaning. The scrapers are made from old files of all lengths and shapes. One edge is hammered flat and ground to a chisel edge, while the other end is bent to nearly a right-angle before it is ground. Shown in Fig. 16.

The brooms are improved by a small scraper inserted in the handle, as shown in Fig 17.

Be sure and keep a large stock of file scrapers, sharpened and ready for use, always on hand, but also keep them all under lock and key till wanted in cleaning up.

We will now start with a mill newly built and note the final preparations necessary before the run is begun. We put a half inch of dry sand in the mortars and place the dies, the sand being required to act as a cushion to the blows of the stamps to prevent the cracking of either the mortar itself or the dies. Then the shoes are placed on top of the dies, the shank being surrounded with soft pine wedges tied on with a string.

HINTS ON AMALGAMATION.

In case the mill is a very large one, say of 40 to 80 stamps, much time is saved by preparing this circle of wedges beforehand. It is done in this way: A shoe is taken and the wedges placed around it, and then a strip of cloth is stretched over them and fastened to each wedge with a tack. This circle is then withdrawn and a sufficient number made for all possible use. After that, it is only necessary to slip one of these circles over the shank of the shoe, and it is at once ready. After the shoes are ready they are driven on singly, by the power employed, a board being placed between the shoe and the die, to eliminate any danger of chipping the iron. They are then hung up by the fingers on the cam shaft floor. The chuck-block is taken to the clean-up room and amalgamated. First, it is thoroughly scoured with a weak solution of nitric acid till the true color of pure copper is shown. Then washed with a saturated solution of cyanide of potassium and quicksilver sprayed from a bottle over the mouth of which a piece of canvas has been stretched. The quicksilver is rubbed into the copper by the exertion mainly of "elbow grease," assisted by a cloth and sand, but it must be very thoroughly attached to the copper, the surplus being removed by one of the "rubbers." The splash plate and lip plate are also dressed in the clean-up room and the operation with them is that which is employed on all the remainder of the plates. They are first thoroughly scoured with cyanide of potassium and then the quicksilver is sprayed over them and rubbed hard with a cloth, avoiding all the use of sand or grit of any kind. Cyanide of potassium is added frequently until the entire surface looks not only bright but wet. Then the surplus quicksilver is again squeezed out with the rubbers and the plates are ready for use.

HINTS ON AMALGAMATION.

The lip plate is now placed in position and the chuck-block keyed to its place and the first section of the apron plate is fastened to the mortar block. Broken ore, both fine and coarse, is now thrown into the mortar and packed around and over the dies to a depth of 2 to 4 inches, when the screen is put in place and the splash plate attended to the last of all. The water is now turned on from two cocks, one on each side of the battery and directly over the tops of the stamp-heads. Two streams are better than one, as it enables us to regulate the proper quantity of water, and also, by increasing the amount on one side or the other to keep the duty of each stamp uniform. Until this water has reached the bottom of the trap do not drop a stamp and then only one battery of five at a time, till it is perfectly under control, both in regard to the feed of ore and the uniform drop of the stamps. At first no quicksilver is added on account of the excess that is on all the coppers, from the preliminary amalgamation. A good deal of this will be carried away by the attrition of the sand and the jar from the battery within an hour, when we can begin to regulate the proper amount and interval of time to feed quicksilver. On average ore we begin with a drop the size of No. 4 bird shot, and as the outside plates gradually get drier, gradually increase the amount fed each time till we find the plates to keep the proper color. All our determinations are made on the splash plate, lip plate and the first few inches of the apron plate.

It is very hard to put on paper the proper color and consistency of amalgam on the plates, but we will do the best we know how. The amalgam on the splash plate and lip plate must be kept hard and dry or very little amalgam will remain there. The first four inches of the apron plate must also be dry, hard and immovable to pressure by the finger, while below it gradually should become softer, and, when pushed by the finger, have the consistency of putty; while at the very bottom of the apron a similarity to thick molasses is not too soft. The color of all must not be dull, like frosted silver, nor as bright as quicksilver alone, but nearly approaches the appearance of a looking glass. Of the two extremes, however, the dull frosted appearance is far preferable, as quicksilver is always being carried by the attrition of the sand and where quicksilver goes there is lost also the fine gold held in solution. The finer the gold, the drier must be kept the plates, the less quicksilver put in at one time and the shorter the interval between the additions of the feed into the mortars. If too much quicksilver is added it is at once noticed from the small amount collected near the battery, and its accumulation increasing as it travels down the plates. When the plates are kept in proper shape near the battery the proper wetness can be controlled at all times, on the lower part of the apron, by an occasional sprinkling of quicksilver, and this will attract the last of the flour gold that may have escaped previous amalgamation without jeopardizing the gold already amalgamated and collected in and near the battery.

Even to-day some people advocate only outside amalgamation, putting no quicksilver at all into the battery, but we believe that as much gold should be caught inside the battery as possible and for flour gold especially the highest efficiency is attained with dry amalgamation in the battery and a soft but not wet amalgamation on the lower apron plate and the sluice plates. Even on ore that runs nearly the same in value, day in and day out, constant watchfulness and observation of the condi-

HINTS ON AMALGAMATION.

tion of the plates must be exercised and it is generally advisable to examine each plate with the aid of a very small stream of clear water each time any quicksilver is to be added. Sometimes a touch of the finger is sufficient to inform the adept, but this takes a long time to acquire, so as to place any trust in it. In addition to observation of the outside plates, daily feel the chuck-block, by removing the canvas over the screen and inserting the arm very carefully. As each watch of men will remove the chips, etc., before quitting time, of course without stopping the mill, they can then feel the chuck-block, see that everything is fastened properly, that the amalgam is accumulating, and has the proper touch and hardness. The touch of amalgam should not be slippery, neither should it be sandy. It must show a uniform hard, dry, and solid surface on the chuck-block, splash and lip plates, but can be moved into a pasty ridge on the apron plate. In regard to the interval of time to allow between the feeding of the quicksilver several factors must be considered. All gold is only amalgamated on its surface, and, therefore, coarse gold requires less quicksilver per value than fine gold, which presents a larger area per unit of value, and, in addition to this, the finer the gold the more frequently the quicksilver must be added. If it is found that the size of the grains of gold in the ore have diminished rather than add the necessary addition to the regular dose reduce the interval of time one-half, or as found most beneficial.

We generally expect on average ore, i. e., $8 to $10 of moderate coarseness, to feed quicksilver once every hour, but if very fine and floured, once every half-hour is not too often. The superintendent must allow some discretion to his amalgamators, as even on ore of very uniform quality it is not politic to give an order for a

HINTS ON AMALGAMATION.

certain feed of quicksilver for more than two hours, and, therefore, it is very necessary that thoroughly competent men alone be employed in this capacity.

We feed the quicksilver and know it is in its best condition, but our labor is lost unless we keep it in that condition as far as possible all the time. Our watchfulness has prevented its contamination by grease and yet, in many cases, even after only a few hours' run, we find the plates coated with various colors that would sicken any subsequent amalgam or quicksilver, so that it will not be attached, but flows on to waste. This coating must be removed, even if the mill is stopped every three hours to "dress the plates."

If the amalgam is removed from the plates too frequently or too close, the silver coating disappears very rapidly and just as soon as the copper is exposed the plates are always tarnished with verdigris, the colors starting as a pale golden yellow, but rapidly becoming dark, greenish and brown. For this there are only two remedies, one to remove the plate and have it re-silvered, and the other, which we consider far better, to amalgamate it with gold amalgam and be more careful in the future from removing the amalgam so thoroughly. First, clean and scour till the pure color of copper is shown with cyanide of potassium, or a solution given later. Then amalgamate with quicksilver, rubbing it in thoroughly and then, after removing the surplus quicksilver, take a little amalgam of floured gold and coat the plate thoroughly with it. Afterward both in dressing the plates and cleaning up, push the amalgam from other parts of the plate to this spot until it is found to keep as bright as all other parts.

With the ores of this State, California, we find a purplish brown stain, caused by telluride of gold, a black or very dark brown, from selenide of gold, and a most beautiful steel-blue sheen which comes from iridosmium. These stains themselves are all rich in gold, and unless saved at the time and place noted, will be mainly lost, as they defy concentration, are apparently soluble in water and, without special chemical treatment, are impervious to the action of cyanide of potassium. It is, therefore, useless for us to use simple cyanide, which, though making the plates and quicksilver bright, would allow all this scum to flow to waste.

There is one mixture, however, that helps us very materially, known to very few, as far as we are informed, and only employed by the two or three possessing its simple formula. Even where there is no special need for its employment we always use it in preference to a simple solution of cyanide. It only consists of a mixture of copperas and cyanide, forming a solution of both ferro and ferri cyanide of potassium.

The preparation of this mixture has never been put in an exact formula, and can either be made freshly each day or in quantity. Our method has been to take two quarts of water and add to it two to four ounces of cyanide of potassium, and when this has partially dissolved, we add a pint of a saturated solution of copperas and stir the mixture thoroughly; but on using this mixture or part of it, we do not clean out the sediment until necessary, but add at first fresh water and the next day more of the different ingredients and fresh water as needed. Crude, but satisfactory results are obtained. The method of application is the same for the daily dressing of the plates as well as to remove stains. The stamps of one battery are hung up, then the water is turned off and the concentrators attached to that battery are stopped, so as to keep their load uniform and

HINTS ON AMALGAMATION.

lose as little of the sulphurets as possible. A stream of clear water of considerable strength is now directed first on the screens and then over the plates till all the sand and slimes are removed.

Starting at the bottom of the first section of the apron plate a whisk broom is dipped into the mixture and the plate rubbed with a circular motion, of which the strongest movement is upwards towards the battery and carries the amalgam that way. This is repeated until the entire section has been scrubbed with the mixture and the whisk broom. The splash plate is then tilted over and the mixture brushed lightly over it, and afterwards the broom is drawn lightly over the lip plate, but any amalgam disengaged is brushed to the apron plate. Very little of the mixture has left the plates and has been acting on the gold bearing stains and the sulphurets which have been attached to the plates by the particles of gold mechanically adhering to them. The plates are now brushed up in a straight line, and all the loose amalgam sulphurets, etc., are collected into a small heap, when they are taken up with a rubber and small iron scoop and put into a china bowl which has some clear water in it. If the lower apron is also stained, it is treated in the same way, but generally the stains are kept on the upper plates. Carefulness has been taken to disturb and remove as little of the amalgam as possible, and most of it is saved in the china bowl; but every time the broom is dipped into the mixture a little amalgam is washed off into the kettle; so that it must all be saved and once a week or so, poured out and cleaned. The amalgam now lies on the plates with microscopic ridges caused by the broom, parallel with the current, and to change these to transverse ridges, the whitewash brush is taken and drawn

HINTS ON AMALGAMATION.

continuously across the plates, back and forth, till the battery is reached, when the water in the battery is turned on, the stamps are dropped and the concentrators started. Generally this treatment is sufficient when done at 7 a. m. and 5 p. m. each day, but as stated above, should the plates again become stained, hang up and dress them in this same way, even as often as every three hours. On no account try to remove the stains with the battery running and the sand passing over the plates, as much amalgam is carried away and the gold in the stains lost forever. Should the plates require dressing every three hours, it is not necessary to rub them so hard with the whisk broom, except in the morning and evening, but this double dressing must not be neglected, even if the plates are apparently clean and bright. They always are improved by it, and with practice ten to fifteen minutes is all that is required on each battery. Whenever it is found that considerable amalgam is collecting at the lower part of the plates, brush it up with the broom towards the head of the plates, and once a week lightly remove the surplus from the lower apron and the sluice plates with a rubber, but do not touch the amalgam on the splash, lip and upper apron till the time for the general clean up of the mill, as the thicker the amalgam that is there, the more of the fine gold is caught and nearer to the battery as well. It is also a fact that gold amalgam is less liable to tarnish than any other amalgam.

We occasionally find another difficulty to contend with, in that the gold is "rusty," that is, coated with a film rendering its surface impervious to the attack of quicksilver. This is of rarer occurrence than imagined, as the loss of gold is very often laid to this cause, when the gold is capable of being amalgamated if proper care and knowledge are employed. In some oxidized ores, taken above water level, a laboratory test of amalgamating will show gold not touched by quicksilver, but here the ore is first ground by itself and then the quicksilver and water (and a good deal of water) are added and it is shaken in a bottle or stirred in a wedgwood mortar, after which the amalgam is separated by panning. In a battery with stamping, coarse gold is hit and cracked and an inside bright surface exposed, which is at once attacked by the quicksilver, present at the same time, before it can again become tarnished; while fine gold is ground temporarily bright by the violent agitation of coarse and fine rock thrown against the sides of the mortar and the screen surface. In this way a great deal of gold, reported as rusty, and not available for amalgamating, is found to act very satisfactorily when actually worked, while this result is helped by the use of our sovereign mixture, the high specific gravity of gold causing it to remain on the plates mechanically, when it is taken up for future treatment in our daily dressing of the plates. If we know positively that we are dealing with rusty gold, we can help ourselves a little by throwing into the battery every hour a piece of bluestone the size of a walnut, but our principal work should be on the outside plates. It is not a very good plan to put any cyanide into the battery, as it may dissolve free gold before the quicksilver has coated its surface or dissolved it.

After the dressing of the plates, the kettle, brooms, rubbers, and bowl of amalgam and dirt, are taken to the clean-up room; the rubbers and brooms are washed, and then put away. If the mill is a small one, ten stamps or less, the amalgam collected at one time is so small, it is better to put the bowl away as it is, and only

HINTS ON AMALGAMATION.

clean the amalgam when sufficient has accumulated to warrant the time expended, remembering that the chemical mixture is acting beneficially and more of the gold is in condition to be recovered. If the mill, however, is 20 stamps or more, enough "muck" (it looks like slimy mud,) is daily collected to make an appreciable quantity of clean amalgam, and this daily amount requires closer manipulation than the large quantity collected on clean-up day. When we find we have enough, including that collected from replacing the screens or any other source, we proceed in this way: First, we have a bowl of quicksilver, kept specially for this purpose and used over and over, because after the first cleaning it has become charged with all the gold it will carry in solution, and we then lose no more from each subsequent daily bath of the new amalgam. The collections from the plates, sulphurets and all, are dumped into this quicksilver and thoroughly mixed with the hand. The dross rises to the top, though a little collects around the sides of the bowl and is mechanically held on the bottom. Placing the bowl in a gold-pan holding some water, we remove the dross and water with a small sponge. After the surface is cleansed, the sponge is pressed to the bottom and sides and all the dross possible brought to the surface and removed, until the quicksilver is bright and absolutely dry. This quicksilver is then poured slowly into another bowl half full of clear water, when most of the remaining dross will be left attached to the sides of the first bowl, and the balance will be floated on the second bowl from which it is removed with a sponge. The dross, with some amalgam, rusty gold and quicksilver, is now entirely in the gold pan, ready for further treatment. This is now put into one of the iron mortars and only a very

HINTS ON AMALGAMATION.

little water kept, not more than a couple of tablespoons full, as we require the mixture to be thick for proper grinding. It is now ground for several minutes, in fact, till it seems to be nothing but a slime, when the mortar is placed in a gold pan, and a stream of clear water under pressure is turned on, the mixture being rapidly stirred with the pestle, till the water flows clear, over the sides of the mortar. The surplus water, except a very little, is then poured off, and the grinding renewed until this clear water is dark and possibly has become thick once more, when the operation of washing with clear water is again employed. After this second washing there should only remain with the amalgam, the iron from the battery and a little coarse sulphurets. Leaving the water in the mortar the iron is removed with the horse-shoe magnet and then the water removed, when the amalgam collected can be carefully added to that in the bowl, leaving the sulphurets behind in the mortar. If this last amalgam still has a bluish or brownish coating, it is a gold-bearing stain and should be added to the general amalgam. The dross, sulphurets, etc., are now put into the copper-bottom pan, which has been amalgamated, shaken in this and washed into the tank.

A piece of the fine canvas is taken and thoroughly wet on both sides and then placed in a bowl of clear water. Into this some of the quicksilver and amalgam is poured, but only a quantity that can be handled conveniently, the canvas is twisted tightly and the quicksilver squeezed through, adding the amount to it, until either it is all in one ball or the ball is of a size not to be cumbersome. Now, it is not necessary to exert great strength to eliminate the last of the quicksilver, as more can be extracted by rubbing the hand or the thumb,

HINTS ON AMALGAMATION.

with a steady pressure over the ball, with frequent immersions in the water, than by violent twisting. When the amalgam is squeezed dry the canvas is laid open on the gold-pan, the bottom covered with water, the ball of amalgam pressed into solid shape, all detached pieces added, and the ball is then rolled over every part of the canvas. In that way it collects every speck of amalgam, and has its surface smoothed with the small amount of quicksilver remaining in the interstices of the canvas, while any dirt or sulphurets is kept from being attached, owing to the water in the pan. Dry amalgam, even with a little free quicksilver, becomes very hard in 24 hours, and the slight addition of mercury to the surface of the ball, from rolling over the canvas, acts as a cement to keep the ball together in a compact mass. The canvas is washed in the pan, squeezed dry and hung up. The floured quicksilver is collected, rubbed by the finger into a globule and added to that in the bowl. The ball is now weighed in avoirdupois ounces, and put into the safe or strong box, and entered into the book for mill reports, as the product for one day or number of days, as the case may be.

It may seem that this work is not required and that the amalgam can be saved and cleaned with that collected from the general clean-up, but it will be found to be money saved, to attend closely to the instructions given above, and particularly where we have to contend with tellurides. The foreman of the mill, or the superintendent of a small plant, have ample time each day to devote to this work; more gold will be acquired, and the retort metal alone, in its cleanliness and the small loss from the subsequent melting, will more than repay the attention to the small details advocated. If this imperfectly amalgamated muck is roughly panned and the amalgam alone saved, the loss in a month is appreciable, and it is forever gone, while this is the only alloy of gold which is hard to clean, and not that from the chuck-blocks or inside the battery.

We see the mint saving the dust on the roof, the carpets, and the clothes of the workmen, and getting a marvelous quantity of gold, and yet, in a mill, the amalgam, the scrapings and refuse are all handled as if of no more value than the sand on the ocean beach. Lately a report was made by a responsible consulting mining engineer, that he estimated the value of an old mill and the ground on which it stood, to be over $40,000.00 in amalgam, quicksilver and sulphurets, and it has been our experience that in the majority of mills which have been in operation for several years astonishing results are obtained from scraping the cracks in the floor and working over everything about the mill or under it as well as the tail-sluice below the property. Save all the chips, screen frames and any wood that has been in use in the battery and sluices, burn them to ashes on an iron plate and amalgamate the ashes. After the castings have become dry, examine them thoroughly, and remove every speck of amalgam, even if some of the iron is broken off with it. Hammer the old screens and scrape off all the rust; while all small bits of iron, even that saved by the magnet, should be mixed with salt and dampened occasionally, and spread out in the sun where it is exposed to the weather. Every six months this is run through the clean-up barrel or clean-up pan, whichever is employed.

The floor, on which are placed the plates, is given a slope towards the concentrators, and at the end of this floor a gutter is placed which will catch all the sweepings and water that may flow down. This gutter must

HINTS ON AMALGAMATION.

have a slight grade, ending in a wooden box or a pipe, to carry off the waste, but in each gutter one or two riffles a couple of inches high, are placed before the overflow pipe is reached. Each morning the plate-floor is swept thoroughly to this gutter, or in summer washed down with the hose, and a stream of water of moderate strength is occasionally run through the gutter, and the concentrated material at the riffles removed. Every leak from the plates is at once calked and stopped, as where the sand goes some of the quicksilver and amalgam will go, even if a panning test might not show an appreciable quantity. We can safely handle all the dirt on this floor, as we have taken especial pains to prevent any drippings of grease, coal oil, or other deleterious substances from coming in contact with the plates or their environs.

One other question has properly to be considered, and that is the temperature of the air, and the battery water, in regard to its action on the amalgam. We see the effect of heat in the expansion and contracton of mercury in thermometers without changing the weight in the least. We also find that our bowl of cleansing quicksilver will have a very appreciable amount of crystalline amalgam after the first cold night. Therefore, we have these deductions to make: As the cold increases, the quicksilver becomes more viscous and slower in motion, and it will not dissolve amalgam, and to increase the cold beyond a certain point the mass is so lacking in its lively characteristic, that it will require more in quantity and with the least beneficial results. According to actual experience this temperature prohibitive to good work is that of 25 degrees Fahrenheit or lower. With an increase of temperature, the quicksilver expands, becomes more fluent, runs easier and will carry much more fine gold in solution, and we are enabled to keep more perfect control over our operations. To any one accustomed to amalgamating "wet," a low temperature will be of most benefit though in no case will perfect work be done. In wet amalgamation the cold viscous quicksilver will form a pasty mass, easily collected with a rubber, but as soon as the temperature rises to summer heat, there is a great divergence between the coarse amalgam and the fluid quicksilver, and, as a result, the upper part of the plates becomes incomprehensibly hard and dry, in spite of an increase in the quantity added, while the more lively and thinned quicksilver runs rapidly off the plates, is floured and lost, carrying with it the increased quantity of gold it is now capable of dissolving, lost forever. As a result, there is a poor efficiency of work that the amalgamator cannot explain even to himself.

In pan-amalgamation of silver ores, the pulp is heated to the boiling point of water, either by live steam, or a false bottom, and all have acknowledged this to be essential even on pure chloride ores, not only on account of the chemical action, but also to put the quicksilver in its most efficient condition. In the cheaper gold amalgamating this can not be done, economically, owing to the steady influx of cold water through the batteries, but common sense will show the benefit of having the battery water as warm as consistent with expense and the health of the employes. In summer, for all practical purposes, the ditch or spring water becomes sufficiently warm in passing through the water-tank and pipes, not to interfere with the efficiency of the quicksilver. But in winter, except in the tropics, the water comes from melting snow, and it is very little above freezing, and unless remedied, it is better to hang up the

HINTS ON AMALGAMATION. 57

mill during the cold weather. In some places it is very dangerous to do this, not only on account of the bursting of pipes, but when once frozen up it will be difficult to start again before warm weather arrives. It is imperative then, to keep the mill moving and thorough preparations should be completed during the early fall,

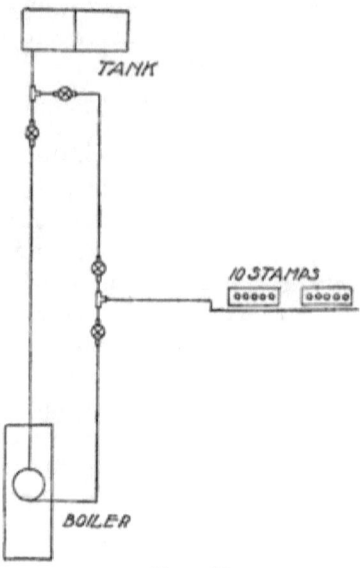

Modern Machinery. Fig. 18.

to provide against a cold snap, even if of rare occurrence. If the mill is run by steam, this is very easily attended to, but wherever possible, mill-power is now derived either directly from water under pressure, or indirectly from water at a distance, driving an electric plant.

If steam is employed, the waste steam is conducted through the water tank, never into it on account of the grease. This is generally sufficient, but in an exceptionally cold locality, rather than add fresh live steam directly to the tank, we advise the following arrangement: Before carrying the water to the battery, pass it through a coil of pipe placed around the steam-drum of the boiler where it will be amply warmed by the waste heat emanating from the surface of the drum. As this will make the water uncomfortably warm in summer, have two sets of pipes, one to go direct to the batteries from the tank, and the other for winter use, leading to the coil. The water leaves the tank in one pipe, but within a couple of feet this pipe enters a "T." With short nipples from the other two outlets and globe valves on each nipple, the water can be diverted either way desired. These separate pipes are jointed together again just before the battery pipe is reached by another "T," the water being under control by two globe valves arranged as in the first instance. Figure 18 will partially explain the plan.

In a mill where the power is either water or electricity, the building is made tight by battening all the cracks, keeping the doors shut, and having all the panes of glass in the windows. Have a large wood stove, at least three feet long, and have plenty of wood, not only for the comfort of the employes, who will attend to their work better, but also for the benefit of the amalgamation. In a cold country it is necessary to have a small boiler solely to generate steam to heat the water in the tank.

In some localities where water is scarce or requires pumping to elevate it above the mill, the water that comes from the mine is used in the battery. This does not require heating unless the reserve tank is very large and the weather very cold. In most mines the drainage water will not hurt the amalgamation, but the acid in solution from the decomposition of the sulphides, and the mud and slimes, are a source of vexatious delays and consequent expense. The acid eats the screens and they break very quickly, and the slimes choke the pipes and soon fill the receiving tank, unless it is very large. Therefore, it is better, if possible, to use spring and surface water in preference to that pumped from the mine, the only advantage of the latter being its uniform temperature the year round.

CHAPTER III.

CLEANING UP.

As the amalgam accumulates in battery and on the plates, a certain time in each month must be taken to remove it all, not only to get the money locked up, but to do the necessary repairing to the mill for a coming run. It is far better to appoint a regular day and adhere to it as near as possible, as the cleaning up when the owner happens to be at the mine, or the superintendent feels like it, always comes when new shoes and dies are not required, and often when the ore is just in the best condition for profitable work in that month. According to the size of the mill and the richness of the ore, this day should be set aside either once or twice a month. Of course, in certain localities it is not advisable, for obvious reasons, to have exactly the same day in each month, and it cannot be too strongly impressed on those in power, to keep the exact day to themselves until the morning that has been set, when instructions are given to the millmen to hang up, and the night shift to work overtime, in the effort to finish the actual cleaning and repairing and start the mill as soon as possible. If the mining property is isolated, with little communication with the outside world, a regular day, once or twice a month, does no harm; but in a community where there are numerous persons unconnected in any way with this particular property, and a section subject to a constant influx and outflow of persons, whether tramps or people

HINTS ON AMALGAMATION.

on special business, it is on the safe side to keep the date secret when the long accumulations are reduced to a portable shape.

For this reason we have advised the preliminary preparations of a goodly stock of scrapers, sharply-cut rubbers, and the making of the wooden wedges for the shoes, to be always on hand and ready at a moment's notice, so that no estimate of the special day can be made from observing the preliminary preparations.

In all mines we find rich ore, medium grade, and poor ore, and an efficient superintendent will try to work all these together in the proper proportions to insure dividends, and yet leave no ore carrying value in the mine. A "tenderfoot" owner will be highly pleased with large profits as long as they last, but is always unwilling to part with some of this profit for future development, when the mine has been robbed of its richest ore. Therefore, it is advisable, in the beginning of a run, to work up for some time the poorer ore of the mine, bringing the product up to a regular amount by extracting more or less of the richest ore as required. Now it depends not only on the size of the mill, but also on the value of the ore, whether the mill is stopped for clean-up once or twice a month. Should all the ore be low grade, we cannot afford to lose any more time than we can possibly help, and should only take one day in each month, as our dies and shoes can be arranged to last that time without renewal. Even if we remove them before their usefulness has ended we make more money owing to the increased production. In a custom mill, after each lot of ore is worked, of course a thorough and general clean-up must be made, as gold ores are not safe to buy outright, with the limited means of accurate sampling which is generally at our service in countries remote from smelters.

In a mill running steadily on ore from one mine, we can afford to allow a little of the value to remain untaken at each clean-up, as it will have an average result in six months or a year, and in reality give more money from a greater production. Most superintendents, on clean-up day, remove all the dies from all the batteries, to get the amalgam in the sand and ore which is packed around them, from two weeks' work, and then replace these partly worn dies for another run. We consider this to be a great loss in a year's run, and a case of greatly mistaken economy for several reasons.

When we first put in the new dies, they were very heavy, and so kept their position, and the tops were absolutely true. Before there was a chance of changing position they became cemented with the rock and sand so as to become an integral part of the mortar. Though the stamps turn at each revolution of the cam shaft, both the shoe and die wear unevenly, but each shoe after a few days will form the greatest crushing surface with its own particular die, in its original position, which has become as fixed as if it were welded to the mortar. This situation will continue till either the shoe or die break from the thinness attained through the steady wearing away of the iron. In addition to this, the quantity of amalgam which settles through this cement will not be of sufficient amount in any one battery, to diminish the total output to such an extent as to be of special moment to secure at that particular time, while in a year's work it will return a much better average. Now suppose partially worn dies are removed, the gravel extracted and the mortar prepared for their replacing. The tops of the dies are now uneven, perhaps worn more on one side than the other, or cupped, but the shoe corresponding to each die is worn the same, and to replace the dies exactly in the same relative position is well nigh impossible, even with the greatest care, and a useless waste of time as well. The result is, that a point or edge of a shoe strikes on a point or edge of a die, offering a minimum of crushing surface for several days, and using up unnecessarily a great deal of iron, with no benefit per ton of ore worked. The lessened weight of the die also allows it to jump from the blow of the stamp, before the gravel has become cemented, and we are specially liable to a cracked die, or, at any rate, one tilted at an angle to its base. After a couple of months at the longest, we find some of the batteries with worn out dies, while others will continue till our next clean-up day. We replace those worn out, and leave the others, after digging out most of the cemented gravel around them, and we get ready for a fresh start in the shortest possible time, and are again making money. We certainly earn no additional money on clean-up day; we only collect that which we have previously earned.

The previous day to that one agreed on, we examine all the shoes and mark those batteries where we have to re-shoe and put in new dies, while other shoes which are too far worn to last a whole run are also marked for removal, and partially worn ones which have accumulated are prepared for these stamps. A close examination is also made of every part of the mill, including the engine, if run by steam, and whether the boilers require cleaning. In the case of steam power, the order to clean up is given the night before, as the mill must be stopped at 4 a. m. to allow the boilers to cool sufficiently to be blown off. A regular system must be drilled into the minds of the employees, so that each one knows exactly what he is expected to do. The firemen attend to the boilers; the engineer cleans and repairs the engine, taking up all lost motion, and then looks over all the line shafts and pulleys, tightening up the bolts on wooden pulleys, relaces or rivets those belts that require it, and does all the other mechanical repairing, assisted by the night engineer. The concentrator men thoroughly clean the machines; go over the plane of the table with straight edge and level, replace all worn out castings, lace the driving belts, and get everything in apple-pie order. The man who attends to the rock-breaker cleans it of all grease and replaces worn out shoes and dies, assisted in this or any babbiting by the engineer. The battery men and all others connected with the mill, who have no special duty, are under the direct supervision of the foreman, and help him, first in removing the amalgam plates to the cleanup room, and then to extract the sand from the batteries, clean off all the amalgam from the aprons and get the batteries in general, ready for as speedy a return to starting as possible, and it is with their work that special instructions must be given.

Orders are given to stop the mill at a certain time, and a few minutes before, the feeders are shut off, and boards put over the throats of the mortars to prevent any more rock being jarred into the batteries. When the stamps begin to strike iron, two methods can be pursued, either hang up all the stamps or reduce the speed of the mill down to about thirty-five drops per minute, and allow the stamps to drop till the water comes through the screens clear, though still carrying some sand. We prefer this last method for several reasons: we have less gravel to handle, the chuck-blocks and all parts of the mortar are clean, and therefore visible, and any quicksilver or amalgam which is in the rock on top of the dies has been thrown out or settled below the tops. The method advocated by some, to hang up all but one battery, and feed this surface rock through it, not only takes a longer time, but requires the workmen to expose themselves to a possible but not probable accident, by working under the stamps with the cam shaft in motion, and they do the work in consequence carelessly, and take a much longer time.

As soon as the stamps are hung up the water is turned off, and preparations at once started to clean up the mill.

First, the splash plates are washed and laid across the lower apron plate. Second, the screens are removed, washed over the plate and carried to the clean-up room. Third, the lower keys are driven out and the chuck-blocks carefully removed and washed over the plates and carried to the clean-up room. Fourth, the lip plate is washed on both sides and placed on the lower apron.

The mill crew is now divided. One man is put in the clean-up room and chisels off the amalgam from the chuck-blocks directly into the tray. A second moves the upper halves of the apron plates down over the lower halves, after thoroughly washing down all the gravel and dirt to the trap. He then scrapes the amalgam from lip plate and splash plate on the upper apron. These two are the day and night shift amalgamators. The others of the crew remove the top gravel from the mortars and dump it into the feeder of one battery. When this top gravel is taken out to the top of the dies the balance of the gravel is picked out around the dies, and those dies extracted which require removal. This cemented gravel is dumped into the barrel or placed in a box alongside of the clean-up pan, and the mortar is thoroughly cleaned, all adhering amalgam on shoes, sides and lip of mortar being chiseled off. The worn out shoes are driven off the stems, and the worn out wedges put into a box for examination and future burning. The new dies are placed in position, and the new shoes with the circle of wedges placed on top of the dies. The partitions are taken out of the traps, the water removed with a sponge and the settlings added to the pulp taken from the battery. The old shoes and dies are washed in a tub, the amalgam roughly chipped off and the sediment added to that in the barrel.

These men now tighten all the bolts around the battery and clean the stems and cams of every particle of grease, using a table knife, coal oil and old sacks. When this is done, wooden blocks are put on the dies, the exact height the drop of the stamps is required to be. The feed stamp is given a half-inch more drop, and the two end stamps a quarter inch more than the others, viz., No. 2 and No. 4, and these stamps are set by their tappets.

The amalgamators and foreman have, in the same time, scraped off all the amalgam from the chuck-blocks and all the plates, and it is stored in kettles and pans, ready for the clean-up barrel; in fact, should be dumped into the barrel as fast as collected to get it out of harm's way. The upper apron is put in place, and the lip plate, splash plate and chuck-block for each battery put on the lower apron. The engine or water-wheel is now started slowly and the shoes driven on, and these shoes are now set by the blocks as the others have been.

All the amalgam and gravel is in the clean-up barrel. Some water and at least 40 pounds of quicksilver are added, though the amount of quicksilver depends on the quantity of amalgam to be cleaned, and sometimes 100 pounds and even more are required. We will explain the use of the barrel first, and afterwards the method of procedure where a pan is employed.

The barrel is placed opposite the door to the clean-up room, in a line with the batteries, and is driven by a belt connecting with the rock-breaker line-shaft. Directly under it is placed a water-tight box 12 inches high, and in the center of this box a worn out die, on which to set one of the enameled pails. On the rear side of this box is an overflow sluice, on which is placed a silvered plate three or four feet long. There are two openings in the barrel, one being a manhole, to dump the material to be worked, and the other a screw plug one inch in diameter, through which the material is drawn on completion of the grinding. To accomplish this attrition there are put into the barrel several pieces of old shafting from one to two feet long, round cannon balls and pieces of broken shoes and dies of all sizes, at least a total weight of 800 pounds. The cannon balls alone do not do either rapid or thorough work, but with the irregularly shaped and sized broken castings, all the ore is quite rapidly ground to a slime.

The cap of the manhole is screwed on tightly, the joint being made quicksilver-proof with a rubber gasket. The driving belt is connected with the pulley on the line shaft, and the engine or water-wheel started. The barrel should not run very fast, as the centrifugal force exerted on the iron and material will hinder the grinding which is done by the rolling of the castings over the pulp. These heavy castings are carried up the side, till their weight overcomes their inertia, when they slide and roll back to the bottom, and a high speed will tend to carry them, if not all the way around, at least so far that they will only drop and not slide over the pulp.

We consider that Mr. Preston makes a great mistake in his treatise, where he advises a speed of 70 revolutions per minute, as this speed should never be over 15 revolutions, and our practice has been to use from 7 to 10, when the pulp is thoroughly ground inside of twelve hours.

As soon as the barrel is started, the night shift go off duty, and if it is late in the day, the day shift remain on duty till midnight. The day shift now dress all the plates with the dressing mixture, thoroughly amalgamate the chuck-block, lip, and splash plates with quicksilver, throw some rock into the battery, replace everything, including new screens, and start on a fresh run. All the implements used are cleaned and taken to the clean-up room, the floor is cleaned and all the mill put in apple-pie order once more.

In scraping the chuck-blocks, we take everything down to the clean copper, but great care must be exercised in scraping the silvered plates, not to go into the silver coating at all. This is not so very difficult, but for this reason the work should be done by the amalgamators, or those who are careful in their operations. There is a great difference in the "feel" of the scraper when going through amalgam or into the silver the latter being very much harder and smoother. In fact it very frequently feels like the surface of glass. The scrapers must have perfectly true edges and be very sharp, with an end like a wood chisel. The flat side is put against the plate and a steady pressure exerted, never a chipping or striking motion. The barrel is allowed to run till there is a steady swish and no grinding is heard. To be on the safe side, it is better not to open it till the next morning when it is certainly ground most thoroughly. The belt is thrown off and the barrel turned

HINTS ON AMALGAMATION.

till the manhole is on top. The cap is removed and washed over the manhole, and the enameled pail (placed on top of the die directly under the screw-plug), and the box, are filled with water from a hose, which hose is fastened to and kept in the pail. The screw-plug is removed, and as the amalgam, quicksilver and slimes flow out into the pail, it is constantly stirred with a wooden or iron paddle, so as to keep the contents in constant

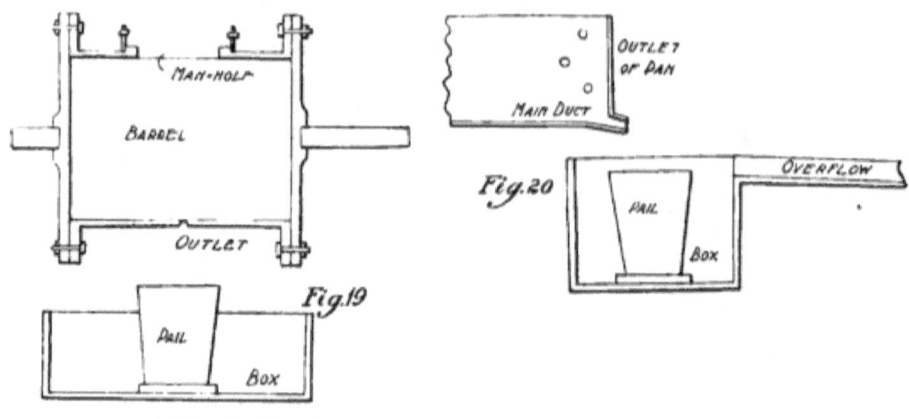

Modern Machinery.

agitation. Whenever no more will run out by itself, the hose is turned into the barrel, and the pieces of iron taken out, each piece being thoroughly washed. All this time the contents of the pail are kept agitated, so that only the heavy amalgam and iron remain, all the sand flowing into the big box and from there over the waste sluice plate. After all the iron is removed, the inside of the barrel is thoroughly cleaned with a broom and the clear water, and our clean-up is finally collected in the pail, but it still requires some work which must now be done by hand. We give a cross section of barrel, pail and box in Fig. 19.

The pail is carried to the clean-up room and the superimposed sand and iron panned in small quantities at a time. The sand is washed away and the iron picked out by hand and extracted with the magnet, until nothing but the quicksilver and amalgam is left. This is squeezed into balls of convenient size, and, with that collected each day, is now ready for retorting. In some exceptionally unsafe localities it might not be advisable to delay the retorting till the day after the clean-up, and in that case all the dirty amalgam is kept separate from the gravel and sand, and is first cleaned by itself in the barrel. In this case there is only need of putting in the cannon balls. The machine will clean and soften the amalgam in less than an hour, when it can be drawn off as described above, the iron extracted and retorted at once. After this is done, all the sand and gravel is put into the barrel, together with the different sized pieces of iron, and is ground till the next day. The amalgam resulting from this is stored in the strong box till the next clean-up.

Though the barrel is more generally used in gold mills, some mill men prefer a grinding pan, which is at all times open to inspection, and can be fed with fresh material without stopping and cleaning out the previous charge. Differing from a silver-amalgamating pan, this one combines the work of both the grinding and amalgamating pan and the settler. The pan should have iron shoes and dies, and three outlets at different heights, closed by wooden plugs, in addition to the main duct set below the bottom of the die. The overflow outlets conduct the tailings directly over a sluiceplate, while the main duct discharges into a water-tight box, fixed with old die and pail. The overflow from this is carried to the same silvered plate that the slimes ran over. This is shown in a cross-section, Fig. 20, which represents only the outlet part of the pan. The speed should be about 30 revolutions per minute, and the modus operandi is as follows: The amalgam alone is first ground with the muller down and a sufficient addition of quicksilver to thin it and only a little water. When thoroughly ground, which should be done in an hour at the longest, water is added, the muller slightly raised, and the overflow plugs opened in succession, with clear water constantly running in till there are no more slimes running out. Then the main duct is opened and the amalgam and quicksilver run into the pail. After all has run out that will, the machine is stopped and the balance swept out with the whisk broom. After the amalgam is cleaned, a charge of the gravel is put in and 40 pounds of quicksilver, and ground moderately, when all that will run down to the lowest overflow plug, after thinning with water, is allowed to escape. The plugs are then put in and it is filled up with more of the gravel. This is continued till all of the scrapings are in the pan. When this is all ground, the main duct is opened at the very last, and the amalgam, quicksilver and iron are run into the pail, and when the iron is separated the amalgam is panned and squeezed.

The advantages of the barrel over the pan are: First, it takes less power to run. Second, it does not require so much skill to handle. Third, it is a thorough grinder and amalgamator. Fourth, the cost of wear and tear is practically nothing, as worn out castings are used. Fifth, its contents cannot be tampered with, unless the machine is stopped.

The disadvantages are: First, it can only be run by hearing. Second, only one charge at a time can be run, and not continuously as in a pan. Third, the separation of sand from amalgam has to be done on discharging the contents, when the pulp is thick and capable of carrying off values.

As the advantages considerably more than balance the objections to it, we would advise the employment of a barrel.

CHAPTER IV.

RETORTING AND MELTING.

The kind of a retort we require in our mill-plant, depends entirely on the amount of amalgam we have to distill at each clean-up. There are two varieties in use, the stationary ones, always used in silver mills, but only employed in gold mills when the amount of amalgam runs over 1,500 ounces; and portable retorts in sizes holding from 30 ounces and upwards. If the number of stamps exceeds 40, and the ore is of good grade, we will require a stationary retort, but its use is of much less importance in general mill work than the portable ones.

Where retorting of large quantities is required, we must have a building entirely separate from the mill. This building will contain one room for the retorting and melting furnaces, and one for the assaying and chemical department, with a small room in which the delicate balances, assay accounts and such things which require care, are kept. The retort is put in the center of the room and the outlet from the fire box extends to a chimney placed to one side. Into this chimney, from the other side come the flues from the two melting furnaces and the muffle furnace. All around the furnaces the floor is covered with iron plates at least four feet wide, the remainder of the flooring being brick set very closely together. The retort is placed horizontally and is closed by a cap covering the whole interior diameter, while the outlet for the escape of the quicksilver, is a small orifice at the top of the rear end, from which it is conducted by a water-jacketed pipe to a receiver, which is an iron tank filled with water. The balls of amalgam are placed loosely in trays which just fit the contour of the bottom of the retort. These trays are first thoroughly coated with chalk to prevent the gold sticking to the iron when softened by the heat. When all the trays are pushed in, the cap is put on and keyed very tightly. Now a tight joint cannot be made with iron against iron, and no gaskets will stand the heat, so we must find a joint unaffected by the heat or the action of the quicksilver. There are several substances at our disposal, and the choice depends only on the presence of one or the other and its relative cost. The luting material can be pure clay, either white fire clay or colored, as the heat is not sufficiently high to melt or even thoroughly bake it. The most common material employed is sifted woodashes, either mixed with water alone or with the addition of salt. Either material is first screened through the 40 mesh sieve, and all lumps in the clay or cinders in the ashes thrown away. A small portion is mixed and puddled with a little water, until it can be moulded in any form without breaking, and yet carries no surplus water. As the puddling is carried on, either water or ashes are added till the right quantity of the proper consistency is obtained. At first a novice is apt to add too much water, the paste seeming to be too dry, but on working it with a knife, it grows softer and more liquid, so that only after considerable puddling and slight additions of ashes is it possible to get it thick and at the same time soft. When ready the cover is laid in a horizontal position and the lute put all around the edge in the recess made for it. It is put on quite

HINTS ON AMALGAMATION.

thick, carefully smoothed with the knife till the surface is perfectly homogeneous, when the cover is placed exactly in its place against the retort and tightly keyed. The surplus lute is squeezed out all around the cover. This is scraped off, and the junction between cover and retort smoothed with the knife.

A small fire of shavings and wood or bark, is now started and the retort gradually warmed, care being used to keep a small fire till all the metal is thoroughly heated. This is to prevent the deflagration of the amalgam, as well as any danger of cracking the retort itself. The heat is gradually raised till the bottom of the retort is a dull red. Then the quicksilver will begin to vaporize. No fuel but wood must be used, and there is no advantage in trying to hurry the distillation. It will take just so long, as there is only a fixed area for its escape in the outlet pipe, and if this is crowded by the pressure of the quicksilver gas in the retort, there is danger of some escaping before the condensation takes place, thus endangering the health of the operator and also of breaking the joint where the condensing pipe is fastened to the retort itself. After the quicksilver begins to collect in the tank, the heat is slightly raised and the retort kept at a cherry red till the amount of quicksilver coming from the pipe slackens up. The pipe is now gently tapped with a hammer occasionally and the fire kept up till no more quicksilver, not even a drop, can be collected on holding the hand under the pipe and tapping it smartly. When this is found to be the case, the fire is allowed to burn out, or is drawn and the retort left to cool. This takes several hours on account of the mass of metal which has been heated so thoroughly.

For this reason, we try to start the fire in the afternoon, and finish the retorting during the night. As soon as it has become thoroughly heated, it is safe to leave in the care of the watchman as no one is able to open the retort or abstract the metal as long as it remains so hot. It is rarely cool enough to open with safety till 7 a. m., the next day, and it should not be touched till the arrival of the one in authority. When ready, the cap is removed and the trays taken out and placed on the iron plates to cool still more. If the retorting has not been done too rapidly and with too high a heat, hard to get with wood fuel, the gold should still be in its pristine balls, now, however, porous and spongy. In the bottom of each tray we always find some of the gold joined together, being partially melted from its proximity to the red-hot iron; but it can be easily broken with a blow of the hammer into convenient weights to handle for the subsequent melting.

At most mines, the amount of amalgam at each clean-up is small in actual bulk, and can be handled with the portable retorts. Each mill should have two on hand, of different sizes, the largest according to the capacity of the mill and the richness of the ore, capable of holding in one charge the total of the clean-up. A retort must never be filled more than three-quarters of its capacity. The danger from over-loading is not appreciated by the average person till a serious accident occurs. Under the influence of the heat the whole mass swells very much, and we have seen, from putting too much amalgam in, first, the complete choking of the outlet pipe by amalgam, and then when the pressure became too great the sudden forcing of several pounds of amalgam with quicksilver vapor, into the receiving tank. In some cases if the retort was old or the cap improperly fastened, a very serious and dangerous acci-

HINTS ON AMALGAMATION.

dent would happen from the explosion of the retort itself.

The portable retorts are in two shapes, those with a flat cover, and those with a curved cover and known as the Nevada retort. The latter style is very much preferable, as it gives, under all circumstances, a reserve space for the quicksilver vapor and allows a little more latitude in filling the retort, besides giving a much stronger keyway and general fastening.

Before putting in the amalgam, every part of the retort must be examined. First see that the pipe is tightly screwed into the cover, and is perfectly clear, tapping it with a hammer and blowing through it. With a new one, be sure and coat it thoroughly, because, if the gold adheres to the iron in any one place, in subsequent cooking with every care taken, it is generally attached to the same place. If the retort has been in use, remove all adhering particles of gold with a chisel and coat most thoroughly. We have a choice of two coatings, one, which we consider the best, is of soft chalk, rubbed on dry from the chunk or powdered, mixed into a paste with water, and plastered smoothly all over the inside; the other, a thin paste of sifted wood ashes and water, which is thoroughly daubed all over the interior. If a paste is used, the retort should be dried before putting in the amalgam. The quicksilver condensing pipe should always be water-jacketed, and can be bought already prepared in this way. This jacket consists of an iron or tin pipe two to four inches in diameter, and made water tight at each end, through which the condensing pipe passes. At the lower end, the furthest from the retort, there is put in a part of a hose coupling to which the hose conveying the cold water can be screwed. At the upper end is a small

78 HINTS ON AMALGAMATION.

outlet, to which a piece of quarter inch pipe is screwed. This pipe is bent and carried down on top of the condenser, discharging into the kettle which receives the metallic quicksilver. If not bought with the retort, any tinsmith or capable engineer can make a tin cylinder of the required size, solder in a hose coupling at the lower end, and solder the whole tightly to the pipe

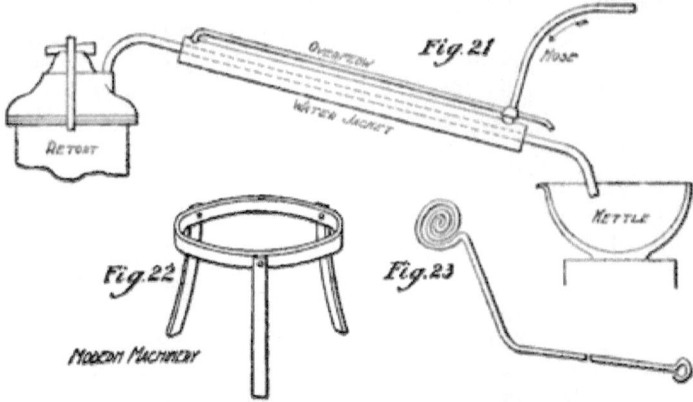

at each end. The constant flow of water will prevent any melting of the solder (See Fig. 21).

Where a water-jacket is used, the end of the outlet pipe is placed a little below the surface of the water in the receiving kettle, an inch being ample. Sometimes it is necessary to use a retort, having only the naked pipe over which water is poured from a dipper. In this case care must be taken that the orifice of the condensing pipe is partly out of the water, and this is very rarely looked into by mill men. The danger of a diminution in the heat consists in the creation of a partial vacuum in the retort, which then sucks up water from the kettle if the pipe is wholly immersed. This water is converted into steam and causes an explosion of great

HINTS ON AMALGAMATION.

danger. With part of the orifice out of the water, only air is sucked up, which causes no sudden increase in the internal pressure; but we are confronted with another danger, that of salivation from the escaping quicksilver gas, unless we close the orifice in some way. Now we wish to impress this point very, very strongly on all those intending to retort the amalgam without a water-jacket. Even if they are fortunate, time after time, in having no serious accident, they will always be more or less salivated, and it takes a very slight exposure to quicksilver fumes to find the teeth becoming loose and other evidences of quicksilver poisoning. The way to prevent it is this: The pipe is wrapped with burlaps or gunny sacks, and a V of tin placed underneath, suspended by wire, to carry the water poured over the upper part of the pipe, away from the fire. This sacking is extended several inches beyond the end of the pipe and into the water of the receiving kettle. In this case the pipe must be straight from the retort to the kettle, with no bend, as shown in the sketch of the water-jacketed pipe. The wet sacking prevents any escape of the quicksilver fumes, and yet part of the orifice of the pipe is out of water. Should a partial vacuum be formed inside the retort, the only effect is to suck the gunny sack against the mouth when the air enters freely through the web.

The retort has been chalked, all parts examined, and the amalgam in balls ready to be packed in it. This packing depends on the subsequent handling of the retort-metal. Where not convenient to melt into a bar at the mine, it is just as well to ship the gold just as it comes from the retort, but in that case we want to have it as compact a mass as possible. If it is melted at once it is better to keep it in its original balls from which the quicksilver has been distilled. When the retort metal is shipped, the balls are broken and the amalgam packed with the iron pestle into one solid mass, that around the sides particularly being smooth, so as to leave no thin ridges to break away. When it is all smoothed, a hole is bored in the center to the bottom, with an iron rod, to act as a vent for the escaping gases and to prevent the entire mass from being raised by the pressure underneath before it makes its own vent. In this case also the heat during the last of the operation is raised to a bright red so as to anneal and partially melt the gold and so hold it together. When it is melted on the spot, the balls are put in unbroken, and sometimes each ball is wrapped in a piece of cloth or paper. The wrapping is unnecessary and only a false idea of excessive carefulness, which results in the distillation along with the quicksilver of pyroligneous acid, and this very quickly chokes the condensing pipe and flours the quicksilver, hindering the operation considerably.

After all is ready, the lute of wood-ashes, with or without salt, is mixed and put on the cover, not on the retort; the cover is put in place and keyed tightly, and all the oozing luting is scraped off and smoothed around the joint.

The next question arises, how and where to retort. Retort out of doors, or under an open shed, where there is no danger of fire. Do not use the blacksmith forge, because too much heat is unconsciously given with the bellows, nor a furnace into which the retort is set, as the heat is not under control, while it is hard to remove a heavy and hot retort, and in both these cases no direct heat can be applied to the bottom. Make a tripod with a ring into which the retort just fits, and high enough to allow a good fire place underneath. This can be

HINTS ON AMALGAMATION.

made by any blacksmith, and the only point to be observed is that the legs shall be extra thick and strong, to withstand any bending from the heat and weight. In addition to the welding of the legs to the ring, put one or two rivets in each leg, for additional security. Fig. 22 shows this tripod.

The tripod is set within distance of the water pipe and the retort put in place, the hose connected and the receiving kettle, partially filled with water, is put at a slight inclination with the end of the condensing pipe submerged in it an inch. A small fire of shavings and a little oily waste is started directly under the retort. This is gradually increased with either pine bark or wood, but slowly until all the air is driven out, and a little quicksilver begins to run. Then the fire is increased and the retort kept at a cherry red till no more quicksilver can be collected, after tapping the pipe. When this is shown to be the case, the fire is withdrawn, the pipe taken out of the kettle, and the cover of the retort taken off. To prove that no more quicksilver is left, take a cold shovel, wet it and hold over the open retort, when it will be covered with a white film if any of the quicksilver remains. Before the retort has a chance to cool, dump out the retort metal into a pan set on an iron plate or directly on the plate, and scrape out any adhering gold. The gold must now be cool enough to handle with the bare hands, before it is weighed, or a correct estimate of its weight is not obtained. It should be porous and bright, or the amalgam has not been properly cleaned.

The question as to what fuel to use is of some moment. Do not use charcoal or coke, even though on account of the greater heat it would be surmised that time can be gained. The top of the retort must be kept as hot as the bottom, and this can only be done with a fuel which gives strong flames. The best fuel is pine bark, but if this is not easily available, dry wood, either pine or other soft wood, will do as well. The wood is sawed into two-foot lengths and split to small size. When the fire is well started, some pieces are placed under the retort between the legs of the tripod, and a complete circle of the wood, placed on end, is stacked against the ring of the tripod, which forms a chimney for draught and a gradually increasing heat. Frequently only one firing is necessary when placed in this way.

The retort metal, if shipped direct, is now wrapped carefully in paper and then sewed and sealed in an ore sack of canvas. If melted on the premises into a bar, we can use the assay furnace, provided there is no special furnace. The fuel used for melting is either charcoal or coke, the latter good English and not gashouse coke. The coke is very much to be preferred. The black-lead crucible, for a long time before use, should be put bottom up on the boiler or other hot place, to get thoroughly dried out. It is then put into the furnace where there is a hot fire dying out. Here it is put bottom side upwards, and left to be annealed till everything is cold. It is then ready for the melting of the gold attended by a minimum of danger as regards cracking. Before the retorting is completed a fire is started in the furnace, and the crucible, resting on a piece of brick, is placed in position. The fire is gradually increased till the crucible is heated almost to a white heat, and the supply of incandescent fuel just reaches to the top of the crucible. The retort metal is now put in from an iron scoop. This can be home made from rolling a thin sheet of Russia iron so that it has a smaller diameter at one end, or a scoop that can be purchased ready made. The crucible is filled nearly to the top with the retort metal, and a tablespoonful of a mixture, containing ground borax and a little sand or ground glass, is at once added. If all of the metal cannot be added at once, the first charge is thoroughly melted before any more is put in. On each subsequent addition a little more of the fluxing material is used. When all the metal is in quiet fusion, the supernatant slag is skimmed off by means of gently passing a coiled rod of cold iron (Fig. 23) over the surface, frequently chilling the slag by pressing it on an iron plate, or slight immersion in water. When the slag is removed, the graphite pot is lifted from the fire and the contents, after thoroughly stirring and mixing with a paddle made from old crucible and heated in fire before use, are carefully poured into a mold already prepared for them. This mold has been first smoked evenly by inverting over a fire of cotton waste, coal oil and pitch or rosin, and then heated as hot as possible by exposure to the heat from the top of the furnace. As soon as the gold has been poured a pinch of candle scrapings is thrown on top and the mold is covered by an iron plate or a piece of wood and left to chill. When solid, but still red hot, the mold is inverted and the gold brick at once immersed in a cold pickle, consisting of water acidulated with sulphuric acid. When cold enough to be handled with the bare hands, it is removed and scrubbed with a brush. Any projections are hammered flat, and the bar is ready for chipping and weighing. Even if no assay is made at the mine, always chip off two pieces from diagonally opposite corners, mark them with date and number of bar, and file away, as a precaution against any future dispute. Stamp on bar number and weight in troy ounces; but it is advisable to abstain from putting on fineness of bullion or its value. In any and all circumstances the buyer will have it remelted and assayed, and it is better for the seller not to publish so widely his own knowledge of its value.

Practically all gold bullion from placers and quartz mines, saved by amalgamation, contains some silver, and this has to be separated before the gold is ready for coining or other purposes. This cannot be done at the mine, and as some gold is lost to the seller in remelting, it is of advantage to ship the bullion as retort metal, save the expense of fuel and the loss in melting. Under any circumstances a fixed charge has to be paid to the refiners.

Louis Falkenau, State assayer of San Francisco, tells us that if the slag dipped off is powdered and panned and old crucibles treated in the same way, there is no loss in melting. And also, if the bar has been properly melted and mixed, the chips will ensure a control which he considers important.

CHAPTER V.

CONCENTRATION.

In the beginning of this series of articles, a rapid summary was given of all the various processes employed in milling that seemed to be of moment. The most minute details have been explained in connection with the extraction of the free gold. We come now to the consideration of the valuable residues still remaining in the pulp, to which the generic name of sulphurets has been given. As the financial standing of gold mining to-day depends exclusively on the ability to extract all the value in the ore, most careful attention is paid to the concentration of these sulphurets at a small expense from the worthless rock into a paying and portable product.

Rival states have waged a bitter controversy over this matter of concentration, contending that each one's special process is the best and should be more largely adopted in other places. We refer to the radical variation in mill practice as pursued in certain localities of Colorado and in California. The author is free to confess that he is prejudiced in favor of the California method, as giving a higher percentage ultimately, in all the sections so far investigated. However, the method must be absolutely correct and not a partial adaptation.

In iron and copper pyrites (the commonest gold-bearing minerals) the majority of the gold is still in a metallic state, microscopic leaves in the fractures of the mineral, and if pulverized to sufficient fineness can be caught with quicksilver, but the expense is increased in a prohibitive ratio, owing largely to the small duty performed by each stamp per horse-power consumed. Again, the sulphurets have been so depleted of their values that it is only possible and advisable to save them where they have more value than the gold they still contain, and where the cost of concentration can be done without additional expense beyond the first outlay in plant. The first condition is obtained by the demand of lead and copper smelters for an iron flux, and their nearness to the mines. This, and this only, has brought the Gilpin county method into a prominence which it does not warrant. Remove the smelters from Denver, and it will be found to be economically impracticable to save the concentrates of that district after the method of milling employed. We are not trying to convert the millmen of that district to our way, but the majority of gold mills have not the good fortune to be in such close proximity to smelters, and it is suicidal to pursue such a method anywhere unless as propitiously situated. The Black Hawk mills save an average of 80 per cent., according to trustworthy sources, and, we honestly believe, this percentage can be raised to over 90 per cent. and at a less expense per ton, if they will stop trying to corrall every speck of the free gold inside the mortar. We wish to be very minute, so that the other districts of the world can judge in regard to the feasibility of the process.

We have mines in this state, in which the ore is very similar to that of Gilpin county, the value all in the sulphurets, which are working over 90 per cent. of the assay value, and at a less cost per ton. Of these the most notable is the "Golden Gate," of Tuolumne county. We would advise any person who is considering the relative merits of the two processes, to make some inquiries

HINTS ON AMALGAMATION.

first, not from the manufacturers of the machinery, but from the owners or superintendents of some of the sulphuret mines in this State. It is not a question of slow or fast drop, but of high or low discharge, and the fineness of the mesh of the screen.

We are all trying to save as much of the value in the mill as possible and at a minimum of expense, and to do this we have to harmonize the two distinct processes of amalgamating and concentrating, and not unduly favor one at the expense of the other.

Now gold has a very high specific gravity and yet becomes so fine that it floats. It is also malleable, but not often brittle, and, therefore, is comminuted very little after being freed from its enclosing gangue. Sulphurets, on the other hand, have much less specific gravity, and are always brittle, which brittleness increases directly as their richness in the precious metals. Expose fine sulphurets for an instant only to the air and they will float on the surface of the water for miles or till submerged by the water falling an inch or more.

Go at any time below any of the mills of the Black Hawk district, except immediately after a heavy storm, and the banks of the gulch will be found lined with sulphurets, while in the eddies, all the detritus is composed of pure concentrates. Go below a California mill, properly handled, and only traces are found on panning, and none is seen with the naked eye. The assay of the tailings for each ton in Gilpin county may be low, but the aggregate in a year that can be saved, is so large that it seems almost criminal to allow such a loss to exist. The keynote of this loss is owing to the unnecessary sliming of these very brittle sulphurets. First, the 14 inches or more that the pulp has to rise through, before discharging, keeps all the ore to be struck so many times by the stamps that the sulphurets are ground to a slime and this is secondarily aided by the fineness of the screen openings, but only partially, as we have very frequently had to employ a No. 12 punched-slot screen on California ores, to save all the values. The output of this is as fine as that of a 50-mesh wire screen.

Now, the greatest trouble to be found in concentration, is to save the slimed mineral, and often the slimes are removed with a point box and settled separately in order to make any showing at all satisfactory. It is, therefore, obligatory to crush as coarsely as is consistent with the loss in the tailings, which loss must be located, whether in the sand or slimes. If in the sand, finer crushing is required till we are satisfied we have reached the most practical, that is, economical efficiency. Of course, it is advisable to save all free gold possible with the quicksilver, but not to such an extent as to ruin the concentration of the remaining values. No matter how fine the sulphurets are pulverized, they will still contain free gold, and even after roasting this free metal will not be absorbed by quicksilver; but it is only with a chemical agent that the gold is saved. If impartially considered, all will agree that the object of stamping is to save all possible value in the mill, and the observation that can be made by any one below the mills employing the different methods, should practically prove the advantage of the process employed in this state.

As there are tricks in all trades, there are certain points in regard to the handling of concentrators and their product which will materially add to the efficiency of the work performed. With some styles of machines, a great advantage is gained by sizing the material to be treated with the aid of "spitzlutten" or ascending columns of water under varying pressure, but this is not necessary with a shaking table working without a jar. In fact, unless there is an undue proportion of clay slimes, the side-shake, endless-belt, machine will do its best work on ore just as it leaves the battery screens, and sulphurets will be separated by the machine which require great care and ingenuity to save after its deposition in the concentration tank.

A vanner in perfect working order should show the following state of affairs: First, no jar whatever, on placing the hand on any part of the upper frame; second, a thickness of pulp on the bed below the ore-spreader of ½ inch, slowly flowing towards the foot of the machine, with a smooth surface and no ripples, and this current must not be faster on one side of the machine; third, a sand edging on each side, along the flange of the belt, of equal width and not to exceed 2 inches; fourth, at the foot of the machine, the tailings to escape towards the middle of the belt, leaving the flanges and a small triangular section of the belt free from sand and exposing clear rubber; fifth, the sand to be kept in view up to the rear side of the clear water box, but showing no dry fingers; sixth, the sulphurets to be passing over the head of the machine in bands between the clear water jets and showing absolutely no sand or slimes; seventh, when the belt leaves the concentration tank, that it shall be cleaned of all the sulphurets; eigthth, that the concentrates deposited in the box and saved by the machine shall be also saved by the operator, and not allowed to escape in the overflow water.

First, no jar. In setting up the machine, the posts and sills are mortised and placed in position, with the keys driven in on the outside of each post. Then the shoulders on each post are cut to scant width and full depth; that is, for a 4 foot machine the measurement between posts calls for 5 feet 6½ inches, but the shoulders are cut to give a distance of 5 feet 6¼ inches, and when the lower frame of the machine is put together the bolts are driven in with a sledge, almost cementing frame and posts. If through shrinkage, later on, the machine gets loose, iron or hard wood wedges must be driven in to form a tight joint. The two rollers underneath the machine must have no lost motion, and must not strike the sides of the lower frame. The lost motion is taken up by tightening the two cross tie rods equally. The prevention of striking is accomplished by moving the roller either way till it clears each side. This is done by loosening the nut of the rod, on the side the roller should go, and tightening the nut on the opposite side (the one which is striking). See that the flat springs, on which the shaking table rests, do not strike the lower frame, and where one does, drive in the lower spring support. Take up all lost motion of the end rollers, by the gudgeon caps, and see that there is none also in the journals and brasses of the shaft, nor in the spur wheel and spring crank shaft. Last, but most frequently overlooked, examine each one of the little rollers over which the belt travels, and move the chairs till there is no side motion, but that they will still turn easily, and then fasten each chair by driving a wire nail or two into the upper rail, in front of the chair.

Second, have a proper bed of pulp. Put a straight edge across top of lower frame and with spirit level make it practically level across, and then place machine on dead center. Take a piece of wood just two inches long and place between upper rail and top of each cross piece of lower frame, and raise or depress lower supports by the bolts passing through lower frame, till this wood just passes easily under lower rail everywhere. The small

HINTS ON AMALGAMATION.

roller next to the main head-roller is raised by a piece of wood a half inch above the plane of the table, but all the other rollers, including the foot main roller, must form a perfect plane. To determine this, a string or straight-edge is placed over the second small roller from the head, and carried over the main foot-roller. Each little roller is made to touch this, being raised by having a piece of cardboard put under the chair, or lowered, by cutting out a slight shaving from the rail. Discretion must be employed to change only those chairs that affect the entire table. Place the main driving shaft by the three movable boxes, so that the distance between outside edge of lower frame and inside edge of shaft is exactly 2 inches ¼ and 1-32. The machine is now ready to start. The speed of the side-shake is first tried at 190 revolutions per minute, and the lower ends of the machine equally lowered till the grade is about ¼ inch per foot, while the uphill travel is started with the small leather belt an inch from the small end of the cone pulley.

The pulp is now turned on and allowed to run for 15 minutes, without altering the machine or until it gets its load. If too light, the foot is raised equally on both sides, but generally it has to be lowered, from being too flat. The water is fixed at a minimum, and the sand is brought up to the water box by increasing the uphill travel. Each machine acts a little differently, so each one is separately regulated, till proper grade and uphill travel are attained. This should be all that is required to put the belt in perfect shape. However, at times, we find a wide expanse of dry sand on one side, and a correspondingly swift current on the other, which must be at once remedied. Knowing that everything is in perfect order, this is at first incomprehensible, until

It is observed that the strain is stronger on one throw of the crank-shaft than on the other and the sand is sensitive to the slightest variation. To overcome this, we have two remedies, the first and simplest to remove and bend the spiral drive-spring, at the head of the machine, inclining the point the way the sand is wanted to travel. The second is, to move the entire main shaft, 1-32 to 1-16 inch, in or out, as the case requires; out, if the heavy sand corner is on the same side as the shaft, and in if the reverse is the case.

Seventh. In order to be sure that the belt is cleaned of sulphurets after leaving the main tank underneath the machine, two series of jets are directed against it above and below, and the pipes must be frequently watched to see that the holes do not clog, most particularly during the time when the accumulated deposits are withdrawn, and the water rapidly lowered in the tank till it may not submerge the belt. It is also very necessary to observe when we lower or raise the machine, that the belt is not either raised completely out of the wash water, or sunk so deep as to cause undue agitation. When raised out of the water, the conclusion is obvious. If sunk too deep, the belt and flange throw the water back and forth so violently that it slops over the sides of the box, carrying sulphurets as well as making everything sloppy; but the chief fault lies in the fact that the concentrations do not settle here but are carried away with the overflow water. With the least agitation too much escapes in this way. This overflow contains the richest in value as well as the finest in size of all which is saved by the machine, and this brings us to the consideration of the very important subdivision No. 8, namely, for the operator to collect that which the machine has saved. It is important, but frequently overlooked. The mill is doing good work, according to the assay of the final tailings, but the product does not tally with these assays, owing to lack of care of the concentrates after the machine has extracted them from the pulp. Some minerals, notably nagyagite and black telluride, largely saved by the machine, will float as a scum on the water of the tank, and run away with the overflow unless it is forced under the water, and the same is true in a lesser degree, of all the sulphurets. To overcome this, we always place a piece of rubber belting in a semi-circle, around the inside of the overflow orifice, which extends at least two inches below the surface of the water in the tank. This requires all the material to be thrust under the water before it can escape; but that which does escape should flow through a very long series of dead-water boxes, in which are placed numerous obstructions to the flow. One obstruction is to place cross-pieces at intervals which extend nearly to the bottom of the box; while another obstruction is to frequently transfer the current through a surface orifice to another box in which the current runs in the opposite direction, and the two together are very efficient. A peculiar slime box was lately brought to our observation, in conjunction with a patented slime concentrator, which appears to be of exceptional value, as presenting great obstruction to the flow of the solid material in the water. We append a sketch of this as of interest, only remarking that the wings are removable. (Fig. 24.)

These devices prevent as much loss as possible in the slimed material while the machine is running, but there are other losses to be guarded against as well. Each machine has constantly on its bed a greater weight of sulphurets than is commonly supposed, which remains uniform as long as the pulp flows on it and it is kept in agitation. Stop the machine and pulp and allow the water to run and this accumulated load is rapidly washed into the tail-race, a total loss, unaccounted for by the assays of the tailings, and it is a very great loss as well. So that on stopping the machine temporarily, always turn off the water and when stopping for some time, as during clean-up, always work off the load on

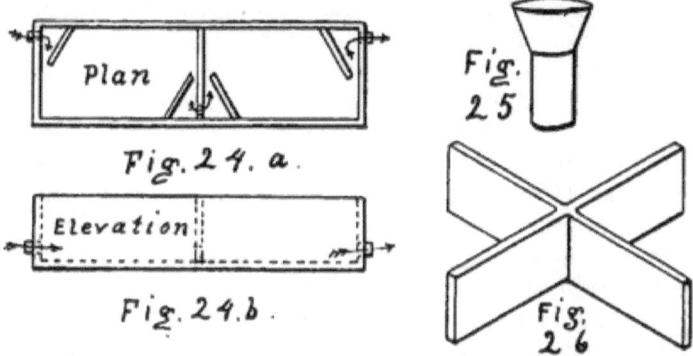

Modern Machinery.

the belt before stopping the machine. A third source of loss is the careless removal of the concentrates. Twice a day the accumulations are hoed out into a drain box, placed in front of each machine, and the surplus water, after settling by blows or stirring, thrown back into the concentration box. Be sure that the wheel-barrow or car is water-tight, and do not fill it more than three fourths full, as in moving it becomes almost a liquid, from the water held in suspension. Have a separate room for storage which is tight, and save all spillings from shoveling, etc., as they count in a year's time.

In spite of the most careful settling, the concentrates will carry at least 10 per cent. of moisture, which should

HINTS ON AMALGAMATION.

be eliminated as a matter of economy if for no other reason. If the sulphurets are chlorinated on the ground, this excess of water increases the consumption of fuel in roasting. Generally, however, the concentrates of one mine are too limited in quantity to warrant the erection of a reduction plant, and therefore, they are periodically shipped to smelter or other custom reduction works. This shipment requires long wagon hauls, besides railroad transportation, for which the expense charges are always based on gross weight. It is easy to see the loss in cash returns on the ore when at least one-tenth, and often one-fifth, of the gross weight is barren water, which can be removed at the mill before shipment with only a little trouble and at a very small expense. If dried as soon as removed from the machine, the sulphurets do not oxidize, clinker and cement together, but allow such a thorough mixing at all times as to get accurate sampling and assays.

The sun is, of course, the cheapest drier, but its use is of doubtful value, if the concentrates are dried on a platform in the open air, as the wind will very quickly scatter several per centum, as soon as they become dry. To use sun heat, a room must be constructed, with the three sides consisting of panes of glass and ventilators in the roof. In other words, have a conservatory without the glass roof. This room need not be very large, as the concentrates, as soon as dried, are shoveled into a storage bin, where they are sacked, sampled, weighed and shipped. For a 20-stamp mill, make the floor 20 feet by 30 feet, putting the room, if possible, on the sunny side of the concentrator room, and place the bin at a lower elevation than this floor.

For artificial drying, very little heat is required, and it can be procured from waste steam, or any scraps of wood chips, etc., that are handy. The top of the drier is made of sheet iron with raised sides. When the sulphurets are nearly dry, they will run like quicksilver on being touched or stirred. In using steam, a coil of pipe is placed underneath the plate, which comes from the engine and which discharges the condensed water and steam outside the building. In using fire direct, it is necessary to build a regular drying furnace, with a relatively large fire-box. The simplest form is to place the iron tray directly on the fire-box, and create the draught with a short piece of pipe at the further end. However, as in all cases it is better to do well anything that is undertaken, we would advise the erection of a regular drying furnace. This will consist of a fire-box and bridge at one end of the plate and a shallow space under the plate from the bridge to the flue, all to be built of red brick and fire clay.

As soon as the sulphurets are dry, they are shoveled into a storage bin, till wanted for shipping. In sacking them the closest woven canvas should be used, and before each sack is sewed a sample is taken with a tryer such as used to sample butter, or made by splitting a half-inch gas pipe. Another satisfactory method is to use a quarter-inch auger. Do not expect any check on the value when a pinch is taken from the top of each sack, as a sample must extend clear to the bottom.

As stated above, the slimes taken from the overflow settling boxes are invariably very much richer than the coarser concentrates which are collected each day, but they are generally very limited in quantity. On account of the small amount, these boxes are only cleaned occasionally, once a month or less frequently. When these are dried by themselves, it is imperative that they shall be uniformly scattered over and mixed with the accumulations already in the storage bin, or the mine is never credited with its full value. If sacked by themselves, the one or two samples taken of them and mixed with the 100 or more samples from the vaster amount of the coarser accumulations, will not be nearly as accurate in giving the average value as if all had been thoroughly mixed in the first place, and the 100 or more samples should each contain their proper proportion of these rich slimes. If the space at the mill will allow it, we would advise sampling as done by the smelters. The concentrates are shoveled into sacks, but every third, fifth or tenth shovelful is put into a separate pile till all the concentrates are sampled. If the resulting pile is still bulky, every other shovel is put into the sacks, and then the remainder is shoveled into a cone, spread out, and quartered down till the assay weight is obtained. With the necessary appliances this can be done very quickly. Beside a broom and square-pointed shovel, there are required a sack-filler, and iron cross for both of which ideas we are indebted to a well known smelter near San Francisco. The sack-filler has been copied from that in use on potato ranches, and is an iron cylinder with a funnel top, which is inserted into each sack. (Fig. 25.)

The iron cross is made of two pieces of iron at right angles, and two sizes should be kept on hand, both in height and circumference. With this cross, each shovelful is dumped directly over the center of the cross, and on smoothing the resulting cone, the quartering divisions are already accurately determined, of uniform size and position. (Fig. 26.)

CHAPTER VI.

SAMPLING.

It is of very rare occurrence to find an assay office attached to a gold mill, but if any intelligent work is done, it is imperative to have absolute technical accuracy at frequent intervals, and not trust entirely to the eye, which is deceptive, no matter how finely trained. In silver mills and other reduction works a qualified assayer who also possesses an insight of the methods in metalliferous chemistry, is absolutely essential to the success of the enterprise. Such wide technical knowledge is not demanded in gold-mill practice, though, of course, of appreciable benefit; but, the superintendent or one of the employes of a company must be able to make an accurate determination by fire of the values in the ore and tailings when required.

Gold is worth $20.67 per ounce, and occurs very irregularly disseminated in the accompanying gangue, when in a free state. On account of its value, a small particle in that piece assayed, might enhance the estimated value of the body of ore under investigation much beyond the working value afterwards determined in practice, and the opposite results might also erroneously be obtained. For this reason, the determination of the value of free gold-bearing quartz in place, by sampling and assay, is a very uncertain method of fixing the value of a mine, and yet it is the one universally employed by experts, and these experts in general, are entirely unfamiliar with the existing conditions of that particular section. As pre-

HINTS ON AMALGAMATION.

liminary information, sampling of a mine and fire assays, are very necessary, but before a definite conclusion is arrived at, wherever possible, a practical mill-test of 25 to 100 tons should be employed, the ore for which is taken from all parts of the mine, without sorting, and just as it would be worked permanently on a large scale. If under no circumstances can such a mill test be made, we advise this method of procedure. The expert comes to the property and makes a rapid survey of the interior workings of the mine, and the character of the wall rocks, strike, etc. Then he will examine the general surface geology of the country, and by inquiry and observation, determine the prevailing conditions of that section. This can be seen by the operations of neighboring mines, if there are any that are working or have been exploited. With the deductions he makes, after sifting out notable inaccuracies due to ignorance or jealousy, it is now with a common-sense foundation of the general conditions that he is able to devote his inquiries to the one mine in view. A few pieces of the ore from different parts are first taken, crushed in a hand mortar, and panned, to determine the character of the gold, whether coarse (when it is probably very unevenly distributed), or fine and floured, which would imply a more uniform dissemination. Of course, the number of samples taken must be in great abundance, near together, and each of large size, and the maximum distance between samples should not be over 8 to 9 feet.

If fine, and several hundred feet of quartz have been exposed, we are generally safe in an average value, if the samples are taken every 20 feet. In every case, each sample must be taken completely across the ledge, either by blast or maul, and everything mixed and quartered down to the size required without using any dis cretion or selection, as that is the way it would be practically worked in a mill. If practicable, have a small assay crusher, and reduce the coarse uniformly, as the quartering proceeds, thoroughly mixing after each reduction in the size of the pieces. A diagram of the mine where each place is sampled, with its corresponding number, is entered in the note book, and the samples are sacked and sent to the assayer for tests, but each sample should weigh 5 pounds, and 15 pounds is better. We wish to state at this point that the value of a mine is not always determined by sampling, but it is the only resource on which an expert foreign to the conditions of a certain section, can rely for his first judgment of the property, while it is the natural preliminary to a practical mill-test. Should the vein be too large to admit of taking one sample across its width, a series of samples are taken in each cross-section at absolutely equal distances apart in every case.

After the assayer returns the individual values to the expert, he is able to lay out accurately the length and direction of the ore-shoot or shoots, in the mine, and whether the ledge-matter intervening, has a value that would warrant its exploitation without reducing the total output prohibitively. He now instructs the assayer to take a weighed proportion of each sample, good or bad, that occurs in the ore-shoot, and make a laboratory working-test, on amalgamation and subsequent concentration. This will serve as a guide for a final mill test, but only as a guide, as the mechanical work of the mill will generally give better results than any hand-test made, though only in total value saved, and not necessarily in an increase of either the free gold or sulphurets. Unless frequent and large samples from the mine are taken as stated above, the resultant mill work

HINTS ON AMALGAMATION.   101

will be very disappointing to the owners, and detrimental to the reputation of the expert himself, unless the blame is laid on a supposedly faulty mill. This is frequently done, and very unjustly, if a good amalgamator is in charge. Grab samples of a few selected pieces, judged by the eye, to be both average, poor and the highest grade, can be assayed, and a test of the ore in 25-ton lots run through the mill, and the resulting product be found to be not over 60 per cent. of what was expected from the average of the selected samples, when accusations of dishonesty are hinted at and often expressed. It seems to be an accepted axiom amongst mine owners that "a custom mill will always cheat," when the fault lies entirely with themselves in estimating what ought to be returned, according to the assays of one or two little pieces of rock, and human nature will force them to take, if not the better looking rock, at least, clean ore, neither of which, it is readily seen, can be any criterion of a mass of ledge blasted down and always carrying more or less of the barren country rock which has to be handled with the clean quartz, on which they form their judgment.

I have gone so fully into a matter that does not seem to be pertinent, because, as mentioned above, the mills are generally so unjustly blamed. Several years ago, I was requested by a prominent railroad man, to make a working test in a neighboring mill, on 25 tons of ore from a mine he held under bond. While the ore was being brought to the mill, I was asked to make three assays, one of a highly mineralized piece of rock weighing less than a pound, and supposed to be so high-grade that similar rock was not shipped to the mill, but was sorted out for sale to smelter. The second sample was one piece of about ½ pound weight, taken from the mine and considered about average, while the third sample was their average of this entire lot and consisted of four little pieces of clean quartz. After making the assays and finding the highest grade did not go over $10 per ton, while the average of the three, even including this one, was under $8 per ton, I examined the ore that had already been stored in the bin and was positive it would not stand up to the assays. Therefore, to protect myself beforehand, I informed this gentleman that I wished him to bear in mind a common report that custom mills invariably retained a part of the proceeds for their personal aggrandizement. On the completion of the test, the resultant amalgam netted $3.50 per ton, the concentrates $1 per ton, and the final tailings 35c. per ton, giving a total of $4.85 per ton of ore treated. On making my report the question was immediately asked, why the returns were so low, when the average of the preliminary assays showed $8 per ton; but, calling to my help the previous statement and the required explanation placed the situation most forcibly before this gentleman. It is, therefore, well to have a most thorough sampling of the mine, or trust entirely to the samples taken in the mill.

Assays during the steady run of a mining property are rarely taken in California, except in the case of foreign corporations, and it is a very great mistake. The expense of an adequate outfit is very slight, at a maximum price of $500, and the cost of all the assays per month, would make no material difference in the profit, while 'n many cases great losses would be prevented. The common practice is to guess at the value of the ore, and the loss in final tailings, by panning. Though it is not imperative to assay by fire all the ore of a free-gold mine daily, yet an occasional assay of a new stope opened, or

HINTS ON AMALGAMATION.

any change in the character of the quartz is a very great help. This same sample should be panned, and then becomes an approximate guide to the value of the different samples that must be panned down each day by the foreman or in case of a large property, the employe especially appointed for that purpose. In the Homestake property, one man is kept steadily at work panning and estimating the free gold value of over one hundred samples each day. The method employed there, is to weigh out a certain portion of each sample and pulverize it to an impalpable powder in a hand mortar, filled with water, the crushing being done by a pestle attached to a power drill. The resultant pulp is panned, and the values of the gold judged by the eye alone, is entered in the report book. By constant practice, the accuracy attained on that ore is remarkably correct, but the same man on another property would require several assays before he would become as adept in agreeing so closely. Again, this will give only the free gold, and is of absolutely no value in determining the gross amount of gold in the ore, where a fire assay alone can be of any benefit. Therefore, in regard to the ore in a free-milling property, be sure and have occasional assays, and do not trust entirely to the eye.

Coming down to the mill, we find a very different situation where a very close estimate of the value of the quartz can be obtained, often by taking periodical samples from the self-feeders, and always accurately by samples below the plates and adding to the values of the assays, the amount of free gold collected.

Several devices for automatic sampling have been invented, but from the fact that it is the exception to see any of them employed, it is coneeded that ordinary

HINTS ON AMALGAMATION.

hand sampling is as correct, gives less trouble, and is always available. Hand sampling has its points to be observed to insure accuracy and very few appreciate the wherefore that it should be done in one way more than another. To get a sample of the quartz before entering the battery, it must be taken as it leaves the feeder to enter the throat of the mortar. Use a dipper, and see that the same quantity each time drops into it. Be sure and be regular in time, either a half-hour or hour, that each sample is taken, and at the end of the specified number of hours, reduce the whole systematically by finer crushing, mixing and quartering. The reason that the outlet of the self-feeder is the only safe place, is that the ore is here the most thoroughly mixed and crushed to a more uniform size. Car samples are only grab samples, a little taken at random from the top, generally the finer pieces, or, if a coarse piece is taken, too great a proportion for that time. From the car the ore is separated by the grizzly into the fines and coarse, but the coarse is broken by the crusher, and, in passing through the ore bin becomes fairly well mixed with the fines. It is then remixed in passing through the automatic feeder, and, being delivered by that to the battery in such a small quantity and thin stream, all of the ore for that instant is caught in each sample. We consider this sample of small importance, as we get immediate returns from the free gold, and it is only the value locked up in the sulphurets that would probably escape us, which we can only determine after the free gold is extracted. Therefore, the important sampling begins at the end of the plate surface. We have two places at our command, at the inlet and at the outlet of the trap. It is unsafe to trust a sample taken below the lower apron plate as there is always the pos-

HINTS ON AMALGAMATION.

sibility of a little amalgam being broken off in passing the dipper along the edge of the plate. If it can be done and the whole stream covered, the inlet to the trap is the better place, as the outlet may carry more sulphurets than the average at one time or the other. The undercurrent will accumulate sulphurets to a ceratin depth, when the increased pressure will throw them out in a bunch, and the process is begun over again. In taking all these samples, a separate dipper must be kept for pulp, as well as for tailings. No overflow whatever is allowed, and the sample is put in a covered can, while the dipper is thoroughly rinsed out each time. The jar of the mill will very rapidly settle all the solid matter when the clear water is very carefully poured off, allowing none of the slimes to escape. In very exceptional cases it will be advisable to evaporate all this water for a comparative test, but the difference will be found to be imappreciable. At the end of the time set, the resultant sample is thoroughly dried, mixed, quartered down and assayed. Should a regular daily assay be made, which will give a correct weekly average, it is only necessary after pouring off the supernatant liquid, to mix most thoroughly the residual slimes into a consistent mass, and then, while stirring, take out a dipperful and dry that for the assay.

The most important sample, and the only one absolutely necessary in a gold mill, is that of the tailings as they leave the mill. These should be taken each hour from the foot of each machine, and never, under any circumstances, from the waste sluice where there might be a partial reconcentration of the tailings. The dipper is drawn steadily across the foot with no pause at either end where a great proportion of the tailings leave the machine. This sample is settled and manipulated as

HINTS ON AMALGAMATION.

described for the pulp, but at the time each one is taken, a duplicate should be examined by panning, to see the amount of visible sulphurets escaping. The foreman should compare the assays of a sample with a panning test of the same, and after several examples can approximately determine the good or bad working of any particular machine, from panning alone. In making these tests, the color of the sulphurets are so different

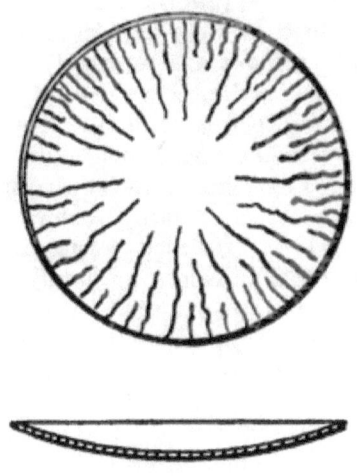

Modern Machinery. Fig. 27.

from that of gold, that they do not show on a dark ground, and they are so fine and light that more care must be exercised, and, in reality, a different method employed. The best color is pure white, and where nothing better offers, a tea-saucer is far preferable to a gold-pan. However, now, there can be procured white enameled pans of all sizes, but choose those with very flaring sides. A patented instrument is now specially made, by which the faintest trace of sulphuret can be detected. The idea originated from the Cornish vanning shovel, used in the tin mines, where all assays are made by hand concentration of the sample. Similar in shape to an ornamental plaque, it is called a vanning plaque. It is a circular segment of the surface of a globe, and is made of wrought iron, covered with a homogeneous coating on both sides of white enamel. The method of using this is different from that of a pan or saucer, in that the plaque is always held nearly horizontal. The tailings are settled by swinging it horizontally and then allowing a wave of clear water to pass over the surface with this same circular motion. When the tailings have been reduced to a minimum without any loss, the plaque is held firmly in the two hands at a steep angle, and by a series of jerky throws, the heavy sulphurets climb up the inclined plane, and can then be collected in a string of colors by gently washing the remaining sand away. (Figure 27.)

In regard to the concentrates, the only reliable assay is of the bulk when prepared for shipment, but a close approximation can be obtained by taking numerous samples with the butter-trier or augur, from the settling box in front of the machine, after the water has been removed. It is unsafe to make any definite conclusion from a sample taken off the belt.

CHAPTER VII.

CONCLUSION.

With the suggestions in the foregoing pages taken as a basis, it should not be difficult for any one to adapt them to the local conditions so as to increase the efficiency of the work, and to correct unknown losses. Put in a concise form, the summary would be.

1st. Beware of grease.
2nd. Amalgamate dry.
3rd. Turn over the pulp as frequently as possible near the battery.
4th. Use all necessary water inside the battery, and do not divide it with a spray outside.
5th. Have the battery water warm, at least above a minimum temperature of 50 degrees, better above 70 degrees.
6th. Use no acids on the plates, nor lye or cyanide inside the battery.
7th. Dress the plates at least one a day, but remove as little of the amalgam as can be prevented till clean-up.
8th. Most thoroughly clean the daily amalgam at once.
9th. Systematize regular clean-ups and do not remove unnecessary dies.
10th. Retort out of doors and do not use charcoal or coke for fuel.
11th. See that the concentrators work noiselessly and without a jar.
12th. Watch the tailings of the concentrators and see that the loss from the mill is kept at a minimum.

HINTS ON AMALGAMATION.

13th. Be very sure that your ore is adapted to the free-milling process.

All gold-bearing ore is not adapted to the free-milling process, and on opening a mine this point must be definitely determined before the reduction works are erected. An assay will determine the value, a panning test will demonstrate if any of the gold is free, and a laboratory working test will inform us of the amount that can be expected to be saved by amalgamation and concentration; but if the final tailings are still very high, some method has to be found to recover this value. Should the highest percentage remain in the tailings, cyaniding must be tried, or chlorination, if the gross value of the ore will stand the expense, while sometimes a combination of all must be used. If the ore is very high-grade and refractory as well, smelting of the mass is the proper procedure. Neither cyanogen or chlorine will economically act on coarse gold, and both processes require crushing. If our panning tests show coarse gold, and the value is too low for smelting, we have to crush, and then, either before or after the chemical work, can secure the coarse gold by amalgamation. The greatest detriment to successful milling is the presence of tellurium compounds, except the telluride of lead and copper. These cannot be amalgamated or concentrated to a practical efficiency, and yet if these ores as usual, show great richness in free gold and coarse gold, they are milled, and, as a consequence, hundreds of thousands of dollars are run to waste, all of which would have been saved if the whole mass had been shipped to a smelter. Therefore, examine the ore for tellurium, and if of sufficient richness, ship, even though at the same time rich in free gold.

In Tuolumne County, California, many of the mines

have chimneys of ore very rich in free gold and tellurides, and the early history of a few of them, show that they were formerly abandoned, though known to be rich, because so little of the value could be saved. One mine can be specially mentioned as a type, namely, the Black Oak. This mine very nearly ruined its owners, by the attempt to work by free-milling alone, was bonded twice and abandoned, and within two years from this time, had been offered on long bond for a small figure. To-day, it cannot be bought, since means have been found to save the $10 to $50 per ton previously lost. No special method has been devised, but reduction was at last adapted to common sense. Instead of using the mill process as the sine qua non, the ore is now partially sorted, the richest shipped direct to the smelter, the balance crushed wet by mill, amalgamated and concentrated. The tailings are impounded and worked by cyanide process, and the concentrates shipped to smelter.

On ores which are purely adapted to concentration, it becomes very frequently a delicate question whether to employ stamps or some other crushing device. In this case, the object is to have the grains of sulphurets, while absolutely freed from the gangue, in as large a size as possible, and with a minimum of slimes. Stamp mills for amalgamating, make a larger proportion of slimed mineral than Cornish rolls and devices of the type of the Chilian mill, for the reason that the pulp will escape from the latter forms, as soon as crushed to the required fineness, while, owing to the height of discharge in a stamp mill, quite a proportion is struck several times before escaping. Here the character of the ore can be divided into two classes: Class A, in which, if it is found that the ore carries enough free gold to pay working expenses, the process as minutely described in

HINTS ON AMALGAMATION.

the foregoing pages must be employed; class B, in which the ore contains no free gold of moment. Stamps are employed on hard ore in which the mineral is finely disseminated through the matrix. The discharge is instantaneous, and the mortar, being merely a crushing device, is patterned after that in use in silver mills. If the ore is soft and shows great tendency to slime, roller mills are the proper machines with vanners to do the concentrating.

The subject is endless, and as a science, gold metallurgy is still in its infancy. However, we trust that the above hints will be of some help in the one branch of this science that has been considered in these pages.

THE END.

www.ingramcontent.com/pod-product-compliance
Lightning Source LLC
Chambersburg PA
CBHW021944160426
43195CB00011B/1221